The Ballboy

True Tales of a Season in the Big Leagues

William Croyle

WEST PARK
PUBLISHING

Contributing editor: Carol Daria.

Front cover photo: Courtesy of The Lorain Journal (The Morning Journal). Photo taken by Larry Burgess, 1986.

Back cover photo: Courtesy of Patrick Reddy.

West Park Publishing logo: Courtesy of Mark and Lorna Reid.

Baseball image each chapter: Courtesy of Moi Cody from FreeImages.

Statistics: Courtesy of www.baseball-reference.com.

First Printing: February 2020
ISBN 978-0-9995238-2-7
eBook ISBN 978-0-9995238-3-4
Printed in the United States of America

To Mom, Dad, Deb, Nick, Dominic, and Vincent.
It took me a while, but it's finally finished.
Thank you for all of your love.

Table of Contents

Introduction

As a teenager, I could crush fastballs with the best of them, but trying to hit a curveball was quite comical. The first one ever pitched to me in a game screamed toward my face at 100 miles per hour, maybe 110. You might claim that I'm exaggerating since the fastest pitch recorded in the history of humanity was 105.1 miles per hour in 2010 by Major League pitcher Aroldis Chapman. But without video evidence to prove otherwise, I'm sticking to my story. With less than a half second to decide if I wanted to live or die, I spun away from the pitch and flopped face down into the ground, taking cover as if a live grenade had been launched my way.

"Steeee-rike!"

Huh?

I peered up from under my helmet and saw the catcher holding the ball, cackling at me through his mask. Parents in the stands snickered, and those were the ones from our team. Even the umpire smirked. Apparently, just before the pitch was about to behead me, it fluidly hooked over the heart of the plate and smacked cleanly into the catcher's mitt, just like a good curveball should.

Batters were just as fearful of me when I was on the mound, though more for their personal safety than my pitching prowess. Nobody, including me, knew where each pitch was going—in the dirt, over the backstop, into someone's crotch. The umpire squatted as low as he could behind the catcher for protection. The batter stood as far away from the plate as permissible, ready to dive out of the way. The catcher, after giving me a pitch sign, made a quick sign of the cross. I didn't pitch often, but it was always an adventure when I did.

The Ballboy

So, when I was 17 years old in the spring of 1986 and my hometown Cleveland Indians issued me a team uniform, it was clearly not to play between the lines. They brought me aboard, instead, to cover foul ground as one of two ballboys that upcoming season. Fortunately, despite my deficiencies at the plate and on the mound, I was strong with the glove. In addition, I worked in the visitors' clubhouse before and after every game, and I served four of those games as the visiting team's batboy. I earned the position through a local newspaper contest, a spirited competition that began with a handwritten essay and concluded with a rigorous interrogation led by arguably the most famous sports journalist in Cleveland's history.

As unparalleled and mind-blowing as that season was for me, I didn't intend to write about it, an obvious observation given that it took me nearly 35 years to finally do it. Though an author by trade, my 10 previous books were written with some of the world's most inspirational people who accomplished incredible feats or overcame insurmountable odds—a paralyzed school shooting survivor, a 9/11 victim who was buried alive for 27 hours, a dying mother who had stage four metastatic breast cancer and knew how life was meant to be lived…

True heroes.

There is categorically nothing inspirational or heroic about snagging a foul ball, retrieving a bat, or dodging chunks of saliva-soaked chewing tobacco rocketing from players' mouths in the dugout. Sure, that last exploit requires quick reflexes, but we all can contort our bodies in some remarkable ways when something that nasty is about to splatter on us. Even the two times I was hit—yes, it was as disgusting as you can imagine—I wasn't afforded any sympathy.

Despite the absence of valor in my job, baseball fans in the decades since have been largely entertained by my stories and have politely pestered me to put them in writing. Once I convinced myself that a nonfiction book can simply be fun without requiring life lessons, I decided to do it.

When people find out that I was on the field and in the clubhouse for every home game, got to know players personally, and shagged fly balls during batting practice—to put just a few of my many experiences in the most general terms—they want to know every detail about the job. How did I get it? What was it like being around professional athletes? Who were the good guys? What superstitions did players have? Were the New York Yankees as arrogant as every Cleveland fan thought they were? What was the clubhouse atmosphere like after a win or a loss? How nervous was I being on the field with thousands of fans watching me when a ball was hit my way? Was anyone ever mean to me?

Yeah, Brad Pitt was.

Well, actually, it was Billy Beane, the player that actor Brad Pitt portrayed 25 years later in the Oscar-nominated film *Moneyball*. Unfortunately, the movie producers and I couldn't agree to terms for them to include my encounter with Billy in their script. Or maybe they didn't return my calls. Either way, the result is that my story, which I aptly call *Meanball*, is exclusively yours.

Though the Indians were the laughingstock of baseball for many years, the 1986 club was relatively good. With the hot bats of Joe Carter and Pat Tabler, the electrifying speed of Brett Butler, Cory Snyder's cannon arm, and the dancing knuckleballs of Tom Candiotti and Phil Niekro—already a 300-game winner and future Hall of Famer at 47 years old—the Tribe finished 84-78 under manager Pat Corrales. That was an astonishing 24 games better than their dismal 102 losses the previous season. They drew crowds in excess of 65,000 for some games, attracted nearly 1.5 million fans on the season (compared to 655,000 the year before), and were in the pennant race through most of August. It was the Indians' best year since 1968.

(Note: In 1986, there were just two divisions in each league. The Indians played in the seven-team American League (AL) East Division that also featured the Yankees, Boston Red Sox, Baltimore Orioles, Detroit Tigers, Milwaukee Brewers, and Toronto Blue Jays. Only the first-place finisher qualified for the playoffs. The way the divisions and playoffs are set up today, significantly watered down compared to then, an 84-78 record could be good enough to qualify a team for a postseason wild card berth.)

This book will follow the season chronologically to give the stories some semblance of organization, though they're naturally more entertaining the further you read. For my fellow Cleveland fans, I will keep you apprised of how the Tribe's remarkable run progressed. However, most of the compelling stories that shaped my experience will be about the visiting players—from guys you've never heard of, to household names—along with some off-the-field personalities. For example, there was that game against the Red Sox when I was responsible for batting champion Wade Boggs going hitless. And the game against the Oakland A's when I single-handedly rescued slugger Jose Canseco's prized bat from the toilet. And the time when *Wheel of Fortune* star Vanna White and I practically became an item during our nearly 20-second pregame encounter, a bond that at least one of us still holds close to the heart today.

I'm not going to get poetic, as some purists and enthusiasts like to do with tales about the game. But baseball—a pastime of imperfections, frustrations, failures, skill, grace, success, glory, competitiveness, and high drama—really does have the power to stir one's emotions. And if my accounts from that season can cause you to smile, laugh, or reflect upon a memorable time in your own life, even for a fleeting moment, then why not share them?

My only regret that season was that my friends didn't get to experience my job. I tried to involve them vicariously by sharing stories with them, leaving them tickets at will-call, or getting them autographs, but it wasn't the same. I wish they all—and any of you who love baseball, for that matter—could have tried it, even just once. From arriving at the stadium a few hours before the first pitch when players asked me to toss with them, to leaving a couple of hours after the final out when I finished cleaning and polishing the last pair of cleats, there was nothing like it. If you had that chance, every detail would be forever imprinted in your mind and heart, as every one of my experiences from that season is today.

Thank you to everyone who hounded me to publish this. I hope you enjoy reading it as much as I enjoyed writing it.

Anything Cleveland

I was raised in Cleveland's West Park neighborhood, about 15 miles from downtown and the Lake Erie shore. We lived so close to the airport that my friends and I stood in our front yards and exchanged waves or other choice hand gestures with passengers as their planes descended.

Our predominantly Catholic community was a melting pot of whites, blacks, Irish, Italians, Slovaks, Germans, Polish, Greeks, and others. Most families, like mine, were considered middle class and lived in modest three-bedroom frame or split-level homes. Others resided in the projects just a mile from my house. I recall my sister's friend who lived there coming over to play one day. She was so captivated by our stand-alone freezer and the treats inside, she repeatedly offered to get me an ice cream sandwich until I finally accepted. I was perplexed by her behavior, so my mom enlightened me. We weren't wealthy by any stretch, but that incident taught me at a young age that wealth is relative; we were fortunate to have what we had.

Our moms were superheroes. They were all homemakers, and several of them also worked outside of the home in an era when that wasn't the norm or even acceptable in some communities and cultures. They were loving and nurturing, yet tough as nails. In the truest test of their superpowers, they could catch wild mice and kill giant spiders that hiked up to our house from the woods behind us. They performed these heroics without flinching, sometimes with their bare hands, leaving us kids in awe.

Our dads, many of them military veterans, worked in a range of professions. Some fed furnaces in steel mills, a few were appliance repairmen, and others were salesmen or pushed pencils behind corporate desks. After serving in the Army, my dad worked his way up to credit manager for a company he started with as a stock boy. Our next door neighbor was an accountant. Our neighbor two houses down was a decorated Cleveland cop. Another one around the corner made his living with the mafia by leading a multimillion-dollar drug ring that had ties to mobsters in New York, Chicago, and Miami.

Really.

When he was finally arrested in the early 1980s, he agreed to testify against his cohorts to help the government convict dozens of them for their drug dealings and killings, essentially dismantling the mafia in Cleveland.

As diverse as our backgrounds and lifestyles were, our differences never divided us. Even the mafia guy drove us to school every now and then, and we played frequently with his children at their house. It was probably the safest home in the neighborhood, given the six-foot-high chain link fence and several full-grown Doberman Pinscher guard dogs that surrounded it. Being neighbors meant being true friends who spent evenings together in conversation on front porches, playing games in the street, or sharing a bond rarely found in neighborhoods today: a perpetual, unconditional, unifying love for every one of our city's sports teams, no matter how awful they were.

If you grew up during or before that era in any sports-crazed town, you understand our passion for any team with "Cleveland" stitched or ironed on its uniforms. The Browns, Cavaliers, and Indians were our three primary professional teams, tightly woven into the fabric of our lives. My grandpa had season tickets for the Browns since 1954 and for the Cavs since they were founded in 1969. He didn't bother getting them for the Indians since there were usually at least 70,000 seats available on game days.

I still have a tattered ticket stub from a game in 1978 between the Cavs and the San Antonio Spurs in the old Coliseum in suburban Richfield—sixth row, center court, a face value of $8.50. At a game today, that might get the front end of your car into the parking lot.

I was 12 when I attended the divisional playoff game between the Browns and the Oakland Raiders in 1981, the year of the "Kardiac Kids." The Browns lost 14-12 after an interception in the end zone in the last minute. It was 37 degrees below zero with the wind chill. I wanted to cry when the game ended, but I was afraid the tears would literally freeze my eyes shut, so I kept my emotions in check until I got to the car.

I was at "The Drive" in 1987, the AFC championship game between the Browns and the Denver Broncos that we lost in overtime, 23-20. That one *really* stung. Denver tied the game on their final drive in regulation and won it in overtime. I was 18, so I refused to cry after that one, but I saw plenty of grown men leaving the stadium who did.

I went to one Cleveland Barons NHL hockey game, on October 19, 1977. The Barons lasted just two years before merging with the Minnesota North Stars, who later moved to Dallas and dropped the "North." The Barons won that game against the Los Angeles Kings, 3-1, in front of about 3,000 fans. My dad and I won the hockey tickets that fall when our "lucky program number" was drawn at a Cleveland Jaybirds/Cincinnati Suds professional softball game. Yeah, the Jaybirds. And it was slow pitch. Seriously, we were all about *anything* Cleveland.

Players back then were heavily involved in their communities and accessible to their fans. Obtaining autographs before and after games was as easy as waiting outside the locker room or next to their cars in the parking lot. They didn't have entourages. There were no private entrances or exits like modern stadiums and arenas have. Few areas were off limits to the public. If a player wanted to get to or leave a game, he had to go through us because he was one of us.

I was outside of the Coliseum after a Cavs game in the '80s when guard Ron Harper was in his sports car and about to leave, but several of us stood in his way hoping to coax him out. Instead of feloniously plowing through us — thank you, Mr. Harper — he turned off the engine, climbed out, sat on the hood, and happily signed autographs for every single person. That was the mutual respect between athletes and fans. And we didn't rush home to hock signatures to make a quick buck. We tacked them on our walls or propped them on our nightstands and ogled them until we fell asleep. Each autograph was an emotional investment and experience, not a financial transaction. How could you not appreciate and love your hometown guys with that kind of personal connection?

The Ballboy

Our main sources of sports information were the Cleveland Plain Dealer morning newspaper, the Cleveland Press afternoon paper, the 6 P.M. and 11 P.M. newscasts on the three or four local TV stations that the antenna on our roof could attract, and whatever we could decipher through the static of AM radio. Sports channels and the Internet that provide second-by-second updates today didn't exist. If you were a transplant from another town curious to know how your team back home fared that day, you had to wait until the 11 o'clock news or for one of the next day's papers to find out. Even then, you were normally provided nothing more than the score. Any details, highlights, or photos were considered bonuses.

I got most of my sports news from the Plain Dealer. Newspapers then were wide, thick, and packed to the edges with stories and statistics. Every morning before school, I ate my Lucky Charms while immersed in the sports section. I analyzed box scores, combed through standings, and digested every quote so that I'd be prepared to talk about it all with my friends. In my last-minute rush out of the house, I often carried the black newsprint to school on my fingers. A nun once yelled at me when she saw my hands.

"Billy! How could you come to school with fingers so dirty?"

"It's just ink from the sports section," I frankly replied.

It was a logical and valid explanation; every household subscribed to a paper. She made me wash my hands, but at least she didn't smack them with her ruler.

The Indians last won the World Series in 1948, 20 years before I was born. They lost it in 1954 after winning 111 games during the regular season. Most of the '60s, '70s, and '80s were abysmal. They didn't return or even come close to returning to the World Series until 1995.

Yet every opening day, like fans of every team, we had hope. Why couldn't this be our year? What was wrong with us thinking in 1978 that Indians' pitchers Sid Monge and Jim Kern could contend for the Cy Young Award with guys like Ron Guidry and Jim Palmer? Or that our double play combination of Duane Kuiper and Tom Veryzer could be the best in the game?

Excitement for the Indians percolated each March when the Browns' season was long over and the Cavs were usually playing for pride. One sure sign that it was nearing baseball season was when the entry form for the Indians' batboy contest was published in the Plain Dealer. The key component to the entry was to write in 100 words or less "Why I would like to be batboy for the Indians." The winner would earn a two-year job: the first season as the batboy for every visiting team that came to town and the second season for the Indians.

That's where this intriguing and improbable adventure begins.

Five Minutes to Spare

Entering the batboy contest for the 1986 season didn't cross my mind all winter. I was a junior at St. Ignatius High School and consumed with academics, extracurriculars, work, and girls. Actually, there were no girls, but I blame that on being consumed with academics, extracurriculars, and work. Those activities, along with the Browns' mediocre season finished, the Indians yet to start, and the Cavs on pace for a mere 29 wins, knocked me out of my routine of perusing the sports section each day. On days when I did read it, I didn't notice the entry form.

On Sunday, March 23, after we came home from Mass, my mom was sitting at the kitchen table reading the paper. The sports section didn't interest her much, but it wasn't unusual for her to scan the Sunday pages to record some knowledge of how poorly Cleveland teams were performing.

"Did you see the batboy contest?" she asked.

"No, I hadn't even thought about it," I replied.

"Well, you'd have to do it right now. It has to be postmarked today."

The Indians opened in Baltimore in just 15 days, and at home four days after that. I was surprised that entries were still being accepted.

"But post offices aren't open on Sundays," I said.

"No, but sometimes there are mailboxes that have Sunday pickup times. We can try to find one. But first, you have to write an essay about why you want to be the batboy."

"I don't think I can write a good essay that quickly," I said.

Mom shrugged. "Anything is possible, but you'll never know unless you try."

The Ballboy

My mom, like most moms, was always imparting her wisdom…when she wasn't busy catching wild mice or killing giant spiders with her bare hands. When she said, "Anything is possible, but you'll never know unless you try," I knew that it was advice I should heed. I also knew that what she really meant was, "I am your mother. I am and always will be wiser than you, and I'm telling you that I absolutely know for certain that you should try this because I know you can do it. If you don't succeed, that's okay; it will make you stronger in the long run. But if you do succeed, it would not only make *you* happy, it would make *me* happy. And you want to make your mother happy, right? But I want you to be the one to figure this out and make that decision."

I usually followed my mom and dad's advice, especially as I got older and realized that they pretty much knew what they were talking about. The times when I didn't listen to them often resulted in regret, leaving me to wonder, "What if…?" At 17 years old I was entering adulthood, which unfortunately is often when the dreams that have danced in our minds throughout our childhood begin to fade in lieu of practical thoughts, such as, "How can I possibly go to school *and* be in extracurriculars *and* have a job *and* look at colleges…*and* girls…*and* be a batboy for a Major League team for an entire season?"

But I knew the answer was as simple as the phrase itself: I would never know unless I tried.

When Mom was finished reading about the Cavs beating the equally hapless Chicago Bulls the night before behind 38 points from World B. Free— my favorite basketball player then and arguably the best name ever—I cut out the entry form and went upstairs to my room. It was about 12:15 P.M. when I began to write. Unlike a couple of my friends who had relatively new, big, bulky devices called "personal computers," I had to resort to paper and pen.

One thing that I've learned about myself over the years is that I often produce some of my best writing when I'm under pressure. I probably have the nuns and their incessant push for perfection while glaring over my shoulder to thank for that. And I guess it's why I have enjoyed being a reporter and author, where meeting tight deadlines is critical to success. However, as a high school teenager, I didn't know that about myself yet, and I was facing what appeared to be three monstrous hurdles: quickly and effectively writing about my lifelong passion for the Indians, doing it in less than 100 words, and finding a mailbox that had pickup on Sundays.

Saying how much I loved the Indians and wanted to work for them had to be the underlying theme of the essay, but I figured every kid would blabber that in the most mundane way. I had to express my feelings at a deeper and more personal level, with a creative panache and without any bunk. What I wrote also had to be real, which meant I probably had to avoid using words like "panache" and "bunk."

Astoundingly, among the thousands of pieces of writing I have produced in my life, I cannot recall a time when the words flowed as freely and eloquently as they did with that essay. I wrote it in 15 minutes straight from the heart. I didn't even have to use any Wite-Out (known today, kids, as the "backspace" or "delete" key).

I stated that I wanted the job because I had an innate desire to be closer to the team. I'd followed the Indians since I was old enough to know who they were, but cheering for them from a distance wasn't enough for me anymore. I wanted to experience firsthand the joy of winning and the agony of losing. Watching them on our 13-inch black-and-white TV, listening to them on my transistor radio, or sitting in the stands was no longer sufficient. I needed to take my love for them to another level.

I also wrote about what the batboy job entailed, based on some inside knowledge I had that I thought might impress the judges. Several years earlier I was in the car with my dad when we were listening to a postgame interview by longtime Tribe announcer Herb Score. He normally interviewed a player, but on this particular day he interviewed the batboy. I was riveted. The batboy shared details about the ins and outs of the job, the hard work involved, and the long hours he put in before and after each game. It sounded like the coolest occupation on the planet.

That last short paragraph you read was 102 words, so you can sense how difficult it was to condense everything into less than 100 words. Some stories I wanted to share, like one about my friend Mark and me imitating the squeaky voice of TV analyst Bruce Drennan during games—and we had his vernacular pegged perfectly—didn't make the cut, but I felt that I squeezed enough solid material into the short space I was allotted to give myself a chance.

It was about 12:30 P.M. when I finished. Mom and I left the house around 12:45 P.M. We lived in North Olmsted, a suburb on the west side of Cleveland, and we were within 15 minutes of several post offices. Mom rolled the dice and picked one in nearby Westlake. She didn't gamble much, but she often won when she did, so I followed her lead. It was 12:55 P.M. when we arrived there. The label on the mailbox outside of the main entrance read: "Pickup: Sundays, 1 P.M." That was the final pickup for the day; we made it just in time. I mailed the letter, dropped off Mom at the airport with a stack of cash and a ticket to Vegas, and I headed home.

I didn't give the contest much thought after that. I was happy with my effort, but the process was so rushed. How could I win against someone who put a lot more than 15 minutes into it? So, you can understand my shock when I came home from school one day later that week and was greeted at the door by my mom bubbling with excitement.

"A guy from the Indians called today!" she exclaimed. "You are one of 25 finalists! You have to go to the stadium this weekend for an interview!"

I was stunned. And ecstatic! How did this happen? I had a lot of questions, but Mom didn't have any answers other than details of when and where I had to report for the interview. Emails and texts weren't things yet, so the guy who called her didn't have time to chat; he had to call 24 other kids with the same message. All I knew, and all that mattered, was that I was still in the running.

I'd like the kids who are reading this to understand something (sorry, I couldn't help but slide a life lesson in here). Before I entered the contest, I believed that I could control every situation I was in, that I was invincible, that I could change anything I wanted to change to suit my needs. Typical teenage attitude, right? Entering the contest taught me that life doesn't work that way. From the word count, to the deadline, to the nerve-wracking interview process you'll soon read about, much of the contest was out of my hands. But I've also learned that, more often than not, the greater effort that I put into something, the more frequently those uncontrollable issues associated with it will fall into place for my benefit.

By putting forth the best possible effort toward everything that *was* within my power—the content of the essay, getting it mailed on time, and mentally preparing for the interview—those things that I couldn't control worked in my favor. There are those who might call that "luck," something that many people told me I had an abundance of after they found out I was a finalist. Call it what you want, but without exerting some of my own sweat, none of it would have happened.

As the late martial artist Bruce Lee once said: "You have to create your own luck. You have to be aware of the opportunities around you and take advantage of them."

Group Interviews Should Be Banned

I went through one formal job interview before the one with the Indians. It was the previous year when I applied to be a scorekeeper and public address announcer at Softball World, a complex of five fields in the suburb of Brook Park. I was hired on the spot, though a job working with beer-guzzling, out-of-shape, middle-aged men trying to relive their Little League glory days in front of their wives or girlfriends whose heads were buried in their romance novels was probably easier to get than one with a Major League team.

I'd also been working for nearly three years at Mazzella Wire Rope, my grandpa's rigging shop, but the "interview" for that when I was 14 was on a Sunday evening in my grandma's kitchen after one of her delicious homemade spaghetti dinners:

"Grandpa, I need a job to help pay for St. Ignatius. Can I work at the shop?"

"Sure. Be there at 8 A.M. tomorrow."

"Okay, thanks!"

Nepotism in its purest form.

My interview with the Indians was surely going to be more difficult. The entry form said that we'd be questioned by members of the Plain Dealer staff and the Indians' organization. But, as my dad so astutely reminded me, I was in the same position as the other 24 finalists. Unless one of them was related to the manager or owner, nobody had an advantage. And if one of them *was* related, I would have no choice but to cry nepotism.

The interview was on a cool but sunny Saturday morning in the restaurant at Cleveland Stadium, home of the Indians and Browns. It was an 80,000-seat monstrosity built at the start of the Great Depression, one of the

17

first multi-purpose stadiums in the country. I wore my church clothes, drove myself there, and walked in about 20 minutes early, yet I was one of the last to arrive. The room, filled with my competitors and some of their parents, was dead silent. Every one of them blankly stared at me, as if I were headless and wearing a Yankees cap on my neck.

What's wrong with you people? I screamed back at them in my mind and with a fake smile. I guess we were all a little anxious. I sat at an empty table in the back of the room. Fortunately, another kid walked in after me and all eyes, including mine, shifted to him. Poor guy. This stare down was seemingly a rite of passage.

The restaurant was large but with a depressing aura, which fittingly matched the Indians' years of futility. It had dark walls, a low ceiling, dim lights, and no windows. This wasn't like a modern restaurant with views of the field. This was in the underbelly of the stadium.

When it was time to begin, Rick Minch, promotions director for the Indians, emerged from a back room and welcomed us. Rick was one of the nicest guys I would get to know in the organization. He was once a batboy for the team and would be promoted later in 1986 to public relations director. His youthful exuberance when he introduced himself relieved a lot of tension in the room, but my blood pressure spiked when he explained the interview process. He said we would be called in five at a time, and he and four others from the Indians and the Plain Dealer would interview us. They would then select the best five candidates overall (not necessarily one from each group) and interview them a second time.

Five of them are interviewing five of us at once? I thought we'd be interviewed one at a time and by two or three people at most. In retrospect, it was unrealistic to expect 25 of us to be questioned on the same day one by one, but I'd never heard of a group interview. Fortunately, among the five groups they interviewed, I was in the second one. That gave me time to digest this bizarre twist and mentally prepare while the first group was being interrogated.

When my group was called in, I walked past three of the kids from the first group as they came out. One was laughing hysterically, one was sobbing, and the other had blood all over his face. Okay, none of that is true. They looked as stoic as when they went in, which didn't help me one bit. I was trying to grab any quick and slight edge I could by reading their reactions to what they'd just been subjected to by the interviewers. Seeing one of them laughing or sobbing—or bloodied—might have helped, but I got nothing.

We filed in and sat in a row of five armless chairs set up side by side against a wall. I was in the middle chair. I barely noticed the kids on either side of me, as I was focused on the five intimidating men in dapper suits staring from behind the table across from us.

I recall three of the five who interviewed us: Rick Minch; Thomas Greer, who was the sports editor for the paper; and Chuck Heaton, one of the paper's longtime sports writers. For an avid reader of the Plain Dealer sports section, I was in the presence of royalty. I'm sorry that I don't remember the names of the other two interviewers. Not to minimize their clout, but it was obvious throughout the interview that the other three guys were running the show.

I knew who Mr. Greer was from seeing his name listed in the paper as the sports editor. And Mr. Heaton? I read his articles and columns religiously. His daughter, Patricia Heaton, who would later become famous for her roles as Debra Barone on *Everybody Loves Raymond* and Frankie Heck on *The Middle*, is one of my favorite actresses—admittedly, in large part, because she is Mr. Heaton's daughter. I was honored to be interviewed by him.

After Mr. Greer welcomed us, Mr. Heaton took charge. He noted that we were all dressed nicely, which he lightheartedly said was something on his list he was supposed to check off. And I did see him make five check marks on his paper; that's how intently focused I was. The score among us after the wardrobe analysis was tied; the competition was already intense. Then Mr. Heaton asked his first question:

"What do you think the job of being the batboy involves?"

Whooooa!

Chills shot through me. This was precisely the first question I envisioned being asked. Recalling that radio interview with the batboy I heard years earlier, this was a lob right over the plate. But there was one *enormous* problem: that "group interview" thing. I was in the third seat. That meant the two kids to my right were going to get to answer the question first.

This was potentially devastating.

I considered stopping the interview to claim that I had dextrophobia—the fear of objects to the right side of the body—so that I could slide over to the first seat, but it seemed impractical. I could only sit quietly, mentally put a hex on my first two opponents, and hope they didn't know what I knew. If they did know, I'd be stuck repeating what they said, which would make me look quite lame.

"Well, you know, the batboy has to go out and get the bat after each batter," Contestant No. 1 said. "And then…"

I was holding my breath.

"…he has to bring it back and put it in the bat rack."

I exhaled.

"Is that it?" Mr. Heaton asked.

Noooooo! I cried in my head. *What are you doing, Chuck?* I was evidently now on a first-name basis with the man I so admired. *Don't ask him if that's it! He answered your question! Move on to the next guy! Please!*

"Yeah, I think that's it," No. 1 said.

Phew! One down.

"So what do *you* think the job of a batboy is?" Mr. Heaton asked Contestant No. 2.

"As he said, you have to get the player's bat and put it away, but you also have to put the helmets away."

"Okay, good," Mr. Heaton said.

"And…I don't know, it's just a lot of hard work."

Mr. Heaton recorded a few notes…and this time, that was it. He obviously heard my earlier telepathic screams, because he didn't offer No. 2 any follow-up questions. Mr. Heaton's eyes then shifted to me.

"And what do *you* think the batboy's job is?" he asked.

It was my moment to shine.

"Getting the bat and helmet and putting them away are certainly part of it, but they are far from everything a batboy has to do. A batboy has to get to games at least a couple of hours early to get the equipment into the dugout and set up. He also has to get the players anything they might need to prepare for the game. During the game he has to retrieve the bats and helmets and put them away, but he also has to get them out and ready for the player before he steps into the on-deck circle."

I was confident that I had politely vaulted myself over my predecessors. Now I had to go for the kill.

"And after the game there is a ton of work to do," I continued. "The batboy has to put away all of the equipment, clean up the dugout, clean and polish the players' shoes, and get the players anything else they need before they leave for the night. He also has to clean up the clubhouse after they leave. Only after all of that can he go home for the evening."

Mic drop. (That's for my sons, who are rolling their eyes at me right now for pilfering their language.)

I vividly recall the warm smiles and nods of approval Mr. Heaton gave me throughout my answer, nonverbally expressing that it was a response far superior to anything he'd ever heard in his life. At least that was my interpretation. I heard the two guys to my right deflate, while the two guys to my left were stuck with basically saying, "Yeah, what he said." I was fortunate that the guys to my right didn't have the vast knowledge about the job that I had, and I felt bad for the guys to my left. I took all the good answers, and they were powerless to stop me. They were victims of a group interview, which I feared for myself going in. This is why group interviews should be banned.

The second question, from Mr. Greer, was about the time commitment to the job and if it would be a problem for any of us. Of course, we all had enough common sense to answer no.

Then came the third question, from Mr. Heaton: "If you were a doughnut, what kind of doughnut would you be?"

"I think I'd be a jelly," Contestant No. 1 said.

I'm kidding.

I don't have a clue what the third question was. My point is that that question and all that followed were fairly irrelevant compared to the first one.

As long as we didn't give any self-incriminating answers, and none of us did, it was clear that the first question would carry the most weight.

When we finished, we returned to the restaurant and patiently waited for the remaining three groups to take their turns. After the last group, Rick came out to tell us that he and the other four interviewers would deliberate for a few minutes. We sat mostly in silence again, still nervous, though I was sure that I nailed it. If for some reason I wasn't selected, I knew that there was nothing more I could have done—other than claim to be the manager's son.

Celebrating with Less than 20 Friends

After three days, Rick finally came out to announce their decisions. Or maybe it just felt like three days because of how skittish we all were.

"The five gentlemen who have advanced to the final round are…"

I don't know which two names Rick called first or which two names he called last. With absolutely no disrespect toward the other four guys, all I heard was, "Blah Blah, Blah Blah, Bill Croyle, Blah Blah, and Blah Blah."

Yeeeeessssss!

That was me yelling in my head, though one kid up front shouted it out loud, eliciting a few chuckles. Who could blame him? We were in the final five! Even though I felt good about my chances coming out of the interview, it was exhilarating to hear my name called.

Rick congratulated everyone and kindly told those who did not advance that they were free to leave. The five of us selected had to return immediately to the interview room. As I headed toward the room trying to keep cool, one of the four guys who was in my initial interview grabbed my arm.

"Congratulations," he said. "You definitely deserve it."

Uh-oh. Another life lesson…

When people say that a random act of kindness can have a lasting impact on someone, believe it. More than three decades later, I still remember what that kid said and the morale boost his five simple words gave me. I thanked him and was now even more poised for the final round. I felt that if I made such an impression on one of my peers, I certainly was ranked high among the final five in the eyes of the judges.

As I continued to walk toward the interview room, I deliberately took my time. I wanted to be the last one in, which would have put me in the first seat to be questioned, based on the previous interview order. But a couple of the other guys were also moving slowly, no doubt on purpose and for the same reason. Not wanting Mr. Heaton to see a fight break out in the doorway as we tried to shove each other in, I picked up the pace and entered the room, cursing in my mind the group interview process. I ended up in the middle seat again.

"Congratulations for being called back," Mr. Heaton said. "This will be our last round of interviewing, but let me first tell you what is at stake. We have five jobs to fill..."

Wait…what? Five jobs? I thought there was only one…

"We have, as you know, the batboy job, which is the only two-year job. The first year you will work for the visiting teams, and the second year you will work for the Indians. Then we have two ballboy jobs for each game; one will sit down the right field line and the other down the left. And you will work with the batboys before and after all of the games in the clubhouses. The other two jobs are alternates. So if a ballboy can't make a game, an alternate would fill in for him. Or, if a batboy can't make a game, a regular ballboy would move into his spot and the alternate would take the ballboy's spot. Does anyone have any questions?"

Yes. Can I give you a great big hug, Chuck? I was blown away! Sure, I still really wanted that batboy job. Not only was it a two-year stint, it included a $1,500 college scholarship. But to have two other opportunities to be part of the team every game was a shocking revelation.

As in the previous interview, I believe it was the first question that decided everything. This time it came from Mr. Greer:

"Let's say you're in the dugout and a player is having a bad game. He can't get a hit, he makes an error, he's frustrated, and he takes his anger out on you by yelling at you or by somehow making your job difficult. How would you handle that situation?"

Gulp.

It was a question that I did not anticipate. Sitting in the third seat now seemed beneficial since it gave me time to formulate an answer. But, ultimately, it didn't matter. The response given by Carmen Tedesco is what I believe won him the batboy job. Not because of his first-seat position, but because of what he said.

"If a player gets mad and takes it out on me, I'm going to tell him to calm down," Carmen stated with authority. "I mean, it's just a game and he shouldn't be treating anybody that way, including me. If he does, I'm not going to back down. I'll tell him he needs to take it easy and relax."

One thought came to my mind when I heard that answer: *Are you freaking kidding me?* And then one more thought came to mind: *ARE YOU FREAKING KIDDING ME?* Same thought, but with more incredulity. And I'm pretty sure I used the word "freaking." Even crazier was that the judges were nodding their heads with approval.

Please don't tell me you guys are buying this! Chuck...Thom...c'mon!

No teenage batboy was going to speak to any Major League player that way in any situation. A more sensible answer, I thought, came from the second contestant who said he would turn the other cheek and do what he could to avoid the player. But I thought his response was a little too far to the other extreme. This gave me the idea to try to find some middle ground.

"If that happened to me," I said during my turn, "I definitely wouldn't confront the player or try to challenge him in any way. It's not my place to do that. But I also wouldn't let his attitude affect me doing my job. If he were in my way, I would find another way to do what I have to do."

I, too, received nods of approval from the panel. I thought that my answer was diplomatic, more realistic than Carmen's, and stronger than the second guy's answer. I thought it also gave me some separation from both of them; our answers were different enough that the judges could clearly make a choice. The last two guys expressed sentiments that were a mix of what the three of us said. It was going to be close; we were five legitimate contenders.

When the interview was finished, we returned to the restaurant and sat quietly while the judges deliberated. I believed that I had a legitimate shot at winning it all, but I was not as confident as I was after the first interview. I didn't believe a word of Carmen's answer to Mr. Greer's question, but there was something about it that made me think he may have edged me out. It only took a couple of minutes before they called us back in.

"You all did a fantastic job," Mr. Heaton said after we sat in our original seats. "You should be really proud of yourselves. It was not an easy decision for us, but here is what we have decided…"

I was trembling inside. A week earlier I would have been thrilled just to have made it this far. But now that I reached this point, I certainly wanted more.

"The first alternate ballboy is…Jim Pauley."

Whoa! I was in the final four.

"The other alternate ballboy is…Eric Rodriguez."

My stomach churned. I forced myself to inconspicuously take a deep breath to try to contain my excitement and not have an asthma attack—or throw up on Mr. Heaton's shoes. No matter what names Mr. Heaton said next, I was guaranteed a Major League Baseball job on the field for every home game!

"Our two regular ballboys will be…Mark Massey and Bill Croyle. Our batboy will be Carmen Tedesco." Carmen exploded with a triumphant "Yes!" and fist pump. Mark and I were each disappointed for about three-tenths of a second before we shifted into celebratory mode. All five of us congratulated each other, and the interviewers shook our hands. I still wanted to give Mr. Heaton that hug, but with the table between us, him wearing that nice suit, and man-hugging not really a thing yet, I gladly accepted his handshake and moved on.

Carmen and I exited the stadium together, and his father was waiting for him outside. The two embraced when Carmen shared the news.

"We're having a party tonight!" Carmen exclaimed to his dad. "Just a small one, like maybe 20 kids."

Wow. I didn't even have 20 friends.

After his dad congratulated me, I got into my car and gave the steering wheel a few quick jabs as I let out an uncharacteristically long and loud victorious yell. I couldn't wait to tell my family and less-than-20 friends! But I *had* to wait, because I didn't have any quarters for the nearby payphone.

I didn't get the job that I wanted, but I got the next best job, which was pretty darn good. I don't know how many entrants there were for the contest, but whether it was 1,000 or 100, I came in second place from among a lot of die-hard teenage Indians fans with the same dream, and for that I was grateful. (Or third place, I guess, if you look at it from Mark Massey's perspective, since our jobs were the same. He can drop me to third in his book if he'd like.)

When I reflected that evening on what transpired at the stadium, I figured out what was so compelling to me about Carmen's answer to Mr. Greer's question: it showed self-assurance and toughness, even a bit of arrogance. The judges probably saw those as essential traits to have when working in a subordinate position to strong, athletic men who are playing a humbling game that can rouse their tempers.

My answer was more pragmatic. In fact, during the entire 1986 season, Carmen didn't argue with or have any confrontations with a single player that I can recall. Yet he still managed to do his job, following the exact answer that I gave. But that doesn't mean his response to Mr. Greer's question wasn't genuine. Carmen was and still is a person of unbridled energy and confidence, and I believe that he believed he would stand up to a player if he had to. I know the judges liked my answer, but they liked his better, and that was easy to accept given my incredible consolation prize.

In less than a week, on opening day, Carmen and I would be on the field with Mark Massey, Dan Rocky (the batboy winner the previous year), and Linda Mancini (she was hired as the ballgirl who sat behind home plate and supplied the umpire with baseballs throughout the game). And we'd all be mingling with the Indians and the visiting Tigers.

I try very hard to never forget where I came from and those who have helped me along the way. There are several reasons why I got that job, but nobody deserves more praise than my mom, whose simple advice I still follow today and impart on my own sons when the opportunity arises: "Anything is possible, but you'll never know unless you try."

"Who Are *You* Guys?"

The only thing better than working opening day is being excused from school to work opening day. The game was scheduled to start in the late afternoon on a Friday, and I needed to be at the stadium by about one o'clock. That meant I got to skip a couple of classes, including my last-period Spanish class. ¡Qué pena!

We were told to enter at the media gate, and Carmen and I coincidentally arrived there at the same time. When we walked in, Indians' long-time equipment manager Cy Buynak was passing through the concourse on his way to the clubhouse. Cy had been with the Tribe since the '60s. He was maybe five feet tall with a giant heart of gold, but a feisty guy. We didn't know who he was yet, but it was obvious by his demeanor that he was in charge of us. I'm not even sure when or if he told us his name.

"Who are *you* guys?" he said with a scowl.

"I'm Carmen; I'm the new batboy."

"I'm Bill; I'm one of the ballboys."

"Where do you guys go to school?"

"St. Ed's," Carmen said.

"St. Ignatius," I followed.

Cy shook his head. "I'm a Benedictine guy!" he replied, his tone conveying that Benedictine was superior to our schools. St. Ignatius and St. Ed's, on Cleveland's west side, are huge rivals academically and athletically. Neither of us knew much about Benedictine, on the east side, other than they had a decent football team. We felt our schools were better in every way, but we weren't about to say that.

Cy stared directly at Carmen.

29

"You! Go down to the visitors' clubhouse!" he ordered, throwing his thumb over his shoulder.

"Where is it?" Carmen asked.

Cy turned around. "It's that door *right there!*" he loudly exclaimed, as if Carmen hadn't seen a door before. Cy was pointing into the distance where we could see a row of several unmarked doors, probably 100 feet away, that all looked the same. Carmen was no doubt wondering which door, but he wisely didn't ask and dashed in that direction.

"And you!" Cy said, looking at me. "What's your name again?" I repeated it. He paused and thought for a moment. "Eh, go with him."

Cy had two options: have me work with him in the Indians' clubhouse, or send me with Carmen to the visitors' side. Initially, I wanted to be with the Indians. They were my team. But when he told me to go with Carmen, I realized that I would get to meet and work with the players from each of the other 13 teams in the AL (unlike today there was no interleague play, the Brewers were in the AL, the Houston Astros were in the National League (NL), and the Tampa Bay Rays didn't exist). I knew that I might not get to know them very well given that each team would only be there for a two-, three-, or four-game series a couple of times that season, but to be able to hang out with some of the greatest players in the game's history for even a brief time was staggering to imagine.

I caught up to Carmen, and we tried to open a couple of doors. One was locked and the other was a storage closet. Fortunately, Cy wasn't watching us, or he likely would have cracked our heads together. On our third attempt, we found the correct one. When we walked in, there was a tiny laundry room to the right. To the immediate left were steps that led down into the tunnel and to the dugout. Also to our left, but to the right of those steps, was a short and narrow walkway to another door. We followed that walkway, opened the door…

And there we were.

The clubhouse.

The small square room had a dirty-orangish floor and aging beige brick walls. Each of the brown wood lockers around the perimeter, maybe 40 in all, were no more than a couple of feet wide and maybe seven feet high. Every locker was identified with a player's name scrawled on white paper and taped above. Understand that the stadium was more than 50 years old. The entire no-frills clubhouse was perhaps 10 to 20 percent of the size of the luxurious clubhouses in newer stadiums today. With a bunch of muscular, adult, male athletes crammed in there, it looked more like the size of a backyard tool shed.

There was a support pillar in the middle of the room with a small color television hanging from it. Next to the pillar was a keg of beer, a garbage can, and an upright glass-door cooler filled with non-alcoholic beverages and tins of chewing tobacco. To the right of the entrance door as we walked in, just past a handful of lockers, was a short hallway. Down that hallway was the manager's office on the right; a small community shower, four bathroom stalls, and a couple of urinals on the left; and a tiny training room straight ahead. And by "training room," I mean it was just large enough to hold two padded training tables where players could get taped before a game, and a one-person metal tub that was more like an oversized beer cooler that a player could soak in after a game. If he could fit.

It wasn't much to look at. But to me, in hindsight, it was like I morphed into the cornstalks beyond the outfield in the movie *Field of Dreams*.

Sitting to my left when I walked in that first time was Darrell Evans, the Tigers' first baseman and reigning AL home run champion, playing in his seventeenth season. A couple of lockers down from him and reading a magazine was Lou Whitaker, one of the best second basemen in the game. Larry Herndon, who hit the go-ahead home run in the first game of the Tigers' World Series championship against the San Diego Padres two years earlier, was next to him.

I continued scanning the room. There was shortstop Alan Trammel, pitchers Walt Terrell and Jack Morris, and catcher Lance Parrish. In 1980, Lance's baseball card was the last one I needed to complete my set that season. After several weeks in search of it, buying countless 25-cent packs of cards at the corner convenience store, I found that my friend Gary had it. Two of them, in fact. I offered to trade him all of my doubles for one, but he was kind enough to just give it to me. I never thought I would find that card, and now here I was in the same room with the player himself.

I stood silently and soaked it all in for a minute. These men were no longer iconic images on a TV screen, descriptions from a radio announcer, or names in a box score. I figured the more I stared at them, the more human they would become, but that didn't happen.

Lou Whitaker! I kept telling myself. *Freaking Lou Whitaker! Right there! That's him!* Meanwhile, Lou was probably saying to himself, *Bill Croyle! Freaking Bill Croyle…*

I was in the midst of my trance when Billy Sheridan, the manager of the visitors' clubhouse, appeared from the training room and snapped me out of it.

"Who are *you* guys?" he said with Cy's same scowl.

No joke. It was the exact same greeting his counterpart just gave us in the concourse. Evidently, the welcoming committee positions were already filled when Cy and Billy applied to work there. This was not going to be a job for the faint of heart. Carmen and I politely introduced ourselves.

"I'm Bill Sheridan!" he replied brusquely, though we would learn that many people called him Billy. "Follow me!" he exclaimed.

He led us out of the clubhouse and to our shared "locker"—the tiny laundry room we passed on our way in. It was something you'd expect to find in the basement of an old house. It had a washer and dryer, concrete floor, unfinished walls covered in cobwebs, a single light bulb hanging above, and barely enough room to stand to throw uniforms into the machines. Billy said we could stuff our belongings each game into the foot-or-so of space between the wall and the dryer. It wasn't the luxury we expected at the Major League level.

"We don't get a locker with the players?" Carmen asked.

Uh-oh.

"A locker?" Billy said in disbelief, his eyes bulging. "You want a locker? When you can hit a 95-mile-an-hour fastball past the pitcher, I'll give you a locker. How's that sound?"

Okay then, no locker.

"Who Are *You* Guys?"

Carmen was given a Tigers' gray road uniform and I was handed an Indians' home white uniform. Though I was working with the visitors, I would be on the field during the game representing the Indians. That occasionally made it awkward walking through the clubhouse, but my five-foot seven-inch, 120-pound stature was a dead giveaway to the players that I wasn't a player from the other team intruding on their space.

After changing into our uniforms, Billy ordered us to carry the bats, balls, and helmets down to the dugout, our first trip into the tunnel. Someone with a severe case of claustrophobia might have struggled to get through it. It was a very long, narrow, cold, damp, dark, rectangular, concrete tube with a thin layer of soiled artificial grass stretched the entire length. But there was no better feeling than walking through it and arriving in the third-base dugout of one of the largest stadiums in the world.

This was where Ted Williams hit his five hundredth home run in 1960, where the Browns beat the Baltimore Colts in the 1964 NFL championship game, where the Beatles performed in 1966, where the Indians played in two World Series, and where the infamous 10-cent beer night occurred in 1974 during a game against the Texas Rangers. Fans that evening got so out of control that the Indians forfeited the game in the ninth inning. Who would have thought that selling beer for 10 cents would cause such chaos?

Carmen and I lugged the bats and helmets to the other end of the dugout and unloaded them into the racks. We then eagerly grabbed our gloves, stepped onto the field, and played catch—until Billy came down a few minutes later.

"What the *hell* are you guys doing?" he yelled. The question was rhetorical for the moment, as he continued to yell. "Who said you could play catch? Where are the coolers of Gatorade? Did you bring down the bucket of gum and bags of sunflower seeds? Let's go! You guys have work to do!"

"Sorry, we didn't know about all that," I said.

"You didn't know? Do you think the players go a whole game without drinking anything?"

Uhhhhhh....

33

Billy and Cy were good men, *very* good men. We had a tremendous amount of fun with them that season despite the stress they were under every game to do their jobs serving the players. They were there early in the day to set up the lockers and do whatever players needed them to do until game time, and they stayed after each game to wash and dry uniforms. They worked 14- to 16-hour days, and Billy oftentimes didn't go home at night; one of the training tables was his bed.

What they did for Carmen and me on opening day was set the tone and expectations immediately so that we could manage ourselves for the rest of the season with little supervision. Though our jobs were dreams come true for us, we were there to work. These professional ballplayers also had jobs to do, and it was our responsibility to make sure they had what they needed to perform at the highest level. There would be plenty of opportunities for fun, but we had to balance it with the labor that was required. I could tell after a few weeks, once Carmen and I figured out our routines and duties, that Billy was happy with our performance, though he never would have admitted it if asked. At the same time, Carmen and I were very comfortable around him, enough that we could reply to his questions and demands with sarcasm and smiles rather than with "Uhhhhhh" and fear.

Since St. Ignatius was on the outskirts of downtown and just a few minutes from the stadium, I started my game-day routine by doing homework in the school library. I then grabbed a sandwich from Wendy's across the street and got to work by about 5 P.M. for a 7:35 P.M. game. Carmen arrived soon after. We got the bats, balls, helmets, chewing gum, sunflower seeds, and some towels to the dugout immediately. We then brought down two large coolers of Gatorade that we made ourselves.

"You get to make the Gatorade the players drink?" a friend at school once asked me.

"Yeah."

"Cool! How do you make it?"

"Ummm…by mixing the Gatorade powder with water and ice."

"Awesome!"

I was serious when I said people were and still are intrigued by every aspect of what my job entailed. If I had told that friend the full and untold story—that it was "cold water" instead of just "water" and "crushed ice" instead of "ice"—his head would have exploded.

Once everything was set for the game, we would return to the clubhouse in case any players needed us. Sometimes they would want us to fetch them food within the stadium or take some baseballs around the clubhouse to have signed by their teammates so that they could give them to friends or family attending the game. Other times they would ask us to get them chewing tobacco out of the cooler that was just a few feet away from them, but that they were too lazy to get for themselves. And that was okay. If a professional ballplayer assigned me a task, no matter how menial, I was happy to do it.

When they headed to batting practice, we followed. Our work during that time entailed chasing fly balls in the outfield, being the cutoff man behind second base, or playing catch with players…if it is fair to call any of that "work." Oftentimes, we would have to sprint up to the clubhouse to get them something they forgot in their locker, such as sunglasses or a batting glove. We did more running before a game than most players did during a game.

After each game we would have to haul everything up to the clubhouse, clean the dugout, and clean and polish every pair of cleats whether the guy played or not. When we were finished, if there was food left from the post-game meal, we were allowed to eat. For a 7:35 P.M. game that took three hours, it would normally be a little after midnight before we were finished working, though we figured out how to work more efficiently and get out a little sooner as the season progressed.

Sometimes we didn't bother eating. At that hour and with school or work the next day, we were anxious to get home. And the food wasn't that great. It featured items such as school-cafeteria-like burgers and ribs that weren't very lean, far below the standards in clubhouses today. Carmen's dad owned an Italian restaurant and made spaghetti and meatballs a couple of times for teams, by far the best meals we had. The demands and timing of everything did not enable us to live the healthiest of lifestyles, but for jobs such as those, we didn't care.

A couple of weeks after we started, Billy asked Carmen and me if we picked up our checks.

"What checks?" I asked.

"Your paychecks."

"We get paid for this?" I asked skeptically.

"Of course you get paid for this!"

I didn't believe him. This had to be a prank, an initiation for the new guys. With no choice but to be certain, Carmen and I walked through the stadium concourse to the office where Billy told us to go. The lady at the front desk had envelopes with our names on them.

Is she in on this joke, too? I wondered.

Still unconvinced that this was real, I opened mine in front of her...and there was a check. My pay was 12 dollars a game. For the time we put in each day, it amounted to less than two dollars an hour. But, considering that I did not expect to be paid at all, I wasn't going to complain. Gas was about 90 cents a gallon. Even after taxes, working a couple of games easily filled my tank, which was a big deal for a teenager.

32,000 Boos

The attendance on opening day was slightly more than 32,000. Coming off a 102-loss season and with the game being on a chilly Friday afternoon, I didn't think the size of the crowd was too bad. The Indians lost, 7-2, stymied by pitcher Walt Terrell, who threw a complete game. After opening the season with three games in Baltimore earlier that week, the Tribe was now 1-3. Late in the game, a couple of Indians fans paraded around the stadium with a giant bed sheet that had the spray-painted message, "Wait till next year." For a city that hadn't won a championship in 22 years in any sport and a team that had the second-worst record in all of baseball the previous year (the Pittsburgh Pirates were worse), the sign seemed fair. It was also funny, considering we still had 158 games remaining.

The Indians' roster looked decent on paper. They had Joe Carter, Brett Butler, Cory Snyder, Pat Tabler, Brook Jacoby, Julio Franco, Tony Bernazard, Andre Thornton, Mel Hall, Otis Nixon, and Andy Allanson, to name some of the position players. Pitching, especially the relief pitching, was the biggest question mark. Starting pitchers included Phil Niekro, Tom Candiotti, Ken Schrom, Don Schulze, Neal Heaton, and, later in the season, rookie Greg Swindell. The bullpen featured guys like Ernie Camacho, Rich Yett, Dickie Noles, Scott Bailes, and Bryan Oelkers.

I sat down the left field line on opening day, but I moved to the right field line the next day and for the rest of the season. The visitors' dugout was on the third base side, and their bullpen was in right field so that they could see their pitchers warm up during the game. When a relief pitcher was summoned, it was the ballboy's job to retrieve his jacket from the bullpen and run it to the batboy so that it would be waiting for the pitcher in the dugout when the inning was finished. Since Mark worked in the Indians' clubhouse and I worked in the visitors' clubhouse, it made sense to switch so that we could continue to serve our respective teams during the game. Obviously, we didn't think of that before the first game.

Our seats were so much closer to home plate than where ballboys and ballgirls are positioned today, which is normally deep in the outfield. Mark and I sat closer to the first and third basemen than we did to the right and left fielders, primarily because the bullpens, as in a lot of old stadiums, were open areas outside of the foul lines. Not only was it our job to retrieve foul balls on the field, we had to help protect pitchers and catchers in the pen, not to mention fans in the stands. In hindsight, we were probably too close (we didn't wear helmets, either), but with Mark and me both being baseball players, we loved it. We were entrenched in the game and always had to be on our toes.

When I got to my position on opening day, there was a Cleveland police officer named John sitting in a chair next to mine. An officer sat along each foul line nearly every game in case any fans decided to run onto the field, which none would that season.

Around the third inning, Detroit's Alan Trammell came up to bat and pulled a hard foul ball well wide of third base. It was coming my way, but it was going to hit the wall first.

My first one!

But I was a mess. It was hit so hard that it took less than two seconds for the ball to travel from the bat to me, though I remember it like it happened in slow motion. My reaction time was spot on, but when I jumped from my chair I slipped on the gravel with my first step. Also, having never played a ball off a concrete wall before, I wasn't exactly sure where to position myself for the carom; if only I paid more attention in geometry class. The ball ricocheted off the wall at a sharper angle than I expected. I lunged to my left toward fair territory, and I could have and should have had it, but I didn't get my glove down. The ball scooted under it and into left field.

As I chased after it like a four-year-old playing in his first t-ball game, trying to get to it before left fielder Mel Hall did, a chorus of 32,000 boos rained down from the stands. For a brief moment, I knew how it felt to be a Major

Leaguer who committed an error in front of his home crowd. I was so embarrassed that I wondered if I was going to be fired. Really, I was scared. They hired me to be a ballboy. My primary job was to catch foul balls, and I failed miserably on my first attempt. Were there repercussions? Was the alternate ballboy going to be summoned to relieve me the next game?

When I sprinted back to my seat, after he was finished booing me with the rest of the crowd, John asked to see the ball. I handed it to him.

"Great, thanks," he said as he dropped it into a black bag on the other side of his chair.

"Are you keeping that?" I asked.

"You and I split them," he said confidently.

Nobody with the Indians told me what to do with the balls.

"Really, we get to keep them?"

"Yep!"

John worked security on the field at the stadium before. He certainly wasn't going to make this up, right?

A few weeks later, when I was in the clubhouse getting a ball autographed by a player before a game, Billy asked where I got the ball.

"I caught it during the game last night."

"You dumb#$%! You aren't supposed to keep those!" he hollered, as if I committed a felony. "You're supposed to put those in the team's ball bag!" Billy called me a dumb#$% that season more times than I can recall. Not nearly as many times as he called Carmen a dumb#$%, but I heard my fair share.

"That's not what the cop told me," I replied.

"The cop? What cop?"

"John. The cop who sat next to me on opening day."

"Oh, so now we're listening to John the Cop about where to put the baseballs?"

"Can I give them to fans?" I asked.

"No! Listen to me! All of the baseballs go in…the…ball…bag!"

I made sure Billy saw me put the balls I caught after the game that night into the team's ball bag. But then the next game and for the rest of the season, I returned to keeping some of them for autographs, and I occasionally sneaked some to fans. I know those sound like risks not worth taking, but I got to know Billy well enough by then to realize that he was just in a bad mood that night and took it out on me. Sure enough, he saw me get autographs on game balls in the days after chewing me out, yet he never said a word about it.

Back to opening day…

A couple of innings later, another ball was softly hit my way. It was a golden opportunity to redeem myself, but the ball was rolling *so* slowly. By the time I ran up to get it, it had come to a complete stop. I bent down, picked it up with my bare hand, and instantly received 32,000 sarcastic cheers. Appreciating their sense of humor, I gave the crowd a quick tip of the cap as I ran back to my seat.

Nobody said anything to me after the game about the error I committed, but I swore to myself that night that no matter how hard a ball was hit my way the rest of the season, I was not going to allow another one to get past me. And I didn't. I sacrificed my body a lot that season and took plenty of lumps on some hard liners, but I didn't hear another boo or sarcastic cheer again.

And I never gave another ball to John the Cop.

No Cleats, No Windshield

You may find this difficult to believe, but none of the batboys or ballboys were offered or required to go through any training by the front office; not a single minute. There was not one meeting. No orientation day. No videos to watch. No handbook to read. We were given no job descriptions. I never met anyone from the human resources department. We learned everything on the go from Billy and Cy.

The only contact anyone from the organization made with me before opening day came in the way of two phone calls I received at home just after I got the job. The first call was from someone asking for my shoe size.

"Eight and a half," I said.

"Great! That's all I need."

Cool! They're buying us cleats!

Another life lesson: don't assume anything, no matter how obvious it may seem. To this day, despite that phone call, I have not received any cleats from the Indians. I wore my own that season, which was fine, but my feet were rather disappointed. I can only surmise that whoever called me had a foot fetish and was curious what the new guy was bringing to the team.

The second phone call was to tell me to come to the stadium to get an ID badge. I went there a few days before opening day and was sitting in the waiting room of their offices when a guy with a beet-red face and tangled hair walked in the door. He looked like he just lost a fight to a vicious raccoon in the parking lot.

"I'm here with Dickie Noles' car," he told the receptionist. Dickie was a new pitcher for the Indians. The guy said he drove it up from Texas, where Dickie pitched the previous two seasons.

41

"You don't look well," the receptionist said with concern.

"Yeah, I drove the car all the way here without a windshield."

"You what?" she exclaimed.

"Bahahaha!"

That was me busting into laughter. Out loud. Dickie's driver whipped his head around and glared at me.

"Sorry," I mumbled as I forcefully reduced my laugh to a smirk. But…c'mon! Really? He just drove 1,200 miles on the highway, much of it in cold weather, without a windshield! Imagine seeing that as a passing motorist! I know it had to be a harrowing trip, but how is that not funny?

As a side note, Dickie's salary that season, according to baseball-reference.com, was $110,000, certainly enough to buy a windshield but a pittance compared to salaries today. The minimum annual salary in baseball in 1986 was $60,000 (equal to about $141,000 in 2020 dollars). The average annual baseball salary then was a little more than $400,000 (equal to about $939,000 in 2020 dollars). Jim Rice with the Red Sox was one of the top earners in 1986 at $2 million (equal to about $4.7 million in 2020 dollars). In 2020, the salary of Los Angeles Angels' outfielder Mike Trout was reportedly about $37.6 million. If you convert Trout's 2020 pay into 1986 dollars (about $16 million), he could have paid Dickie Noles' entire salary in 1986 *and* bought him a new windshield after playing just 11 innings.

My primary takeaway from that opening weekend, aside from trying to learn everything on the fly, was that professional baseball players were very much just like me. They may have been more athletic, financially wealthier, and older—no different than a lot of people I knew—but that was pretty much where the disparities ended. They ate, slept, read, laughed, watched TV, had families, were happy when they did their jobs well, and were upset when they didn't. They were, in general, normal and good people who treated each other and me with respect.

"Sweet" Lou Whitaker was as kind as his nickname. So was Alan Trammell. Dave Collins was my favorite that first series.

"Grab your glove," Dave said to me in the dugout before the second game. Though Billy yelled at me the day before for playing catch with Carmen,

I assumed that if a player told me to grab my glove, it was my job. Dave, who played on eight different teams and at several different positions in a 16-year career, hit some ground balls to me in foul territory during batting practice for about 20 minutes to get himself loose. When we were finished, he asked me where I went to school and what I wanted to do after graduation. It was the first time a player initiated a conversation with me and included me in his pregame warm-ups. Some other big-name players I liked on that team, such as Evans, Herndon, Morris, Chet Lemon, and Frank Tanana, didn't interact with me much, but they were all happy to sign autographs when I asked.

The Tigers' coaching staff was a wonderful group of guys that included Alex Grammas, Billy Consolo, and manager Sparky Anderson. Anderson was previously the manager of the two-time world champion Cincinnati Reds' "Big Red Machine" in the '70s, and Grammas was one of his coaches on that team. Consolo played for 10 years in the '50s and '60s and joined Anderson's staff in Detroit in 1979. They were confident gentlemen and good friends who had fun doing what they did, seemingly taking everything in stride. Win or lose, they appeared relaxed and content in the clubhouse, accepting baseball for the game that it was. I'm sure they got fired up when they had to, but that certainly didn't define their personalities. They were the kind of guys you'd love to hang with, who would likely welcome you into their circle and keep you entertained well into the night with fascinating stories about baseball and life.

Kirk Gibson, the team's right fielder, was the most bombastic player on the team. He was the first player like that whom I encountered, much different from the other Tigers. When he entered the clubhouse, everyone knew it. A former star football player at Michigan State University and a 2017 inductee into the College Football Hall of Fame, he seemed to be on a perpetual adrenaline high. He was loud, funny, and arrogant, cursed like a sailor, and paid no attention to me, which was perfectly okay since I was just the ballboy. But his eccentric behavior and my newness to the job made him intimidating to be around.

The Indians beat Morris and Tanana, two excellent pitchers, in the final two games of the series to even their record at 3-3. Gibson had a decent series at the plate, but he struck out twice in the last game. I got some autographs over the three days, and I really wanted to get Gibson's before he left given how good of a player he was, but with his struggles at the plate and the two losses, I thought it would be best to hit him up when the Tigers returned in July. Besides, I was already looking forward to the Yankees coming to town in a couple of days.

Want an Autograph? Don't Be a Jerk

During the off day between the Tigers' series and the Yankees' series, I went to a local sporting goods store to buy a few dozen plastic baseball holders, assuming that I would be collecting a lot of autographs that season. Obtaining autographs wasn't as important to me as forming relationships with players and staff. Having a genuine conversation with someone like Sparky Anderson who would remember my name the next day was far more exciting than getting a signature. But having been an autograph collector for much of my childhood, it was certainly a golden opportunity I didn't want to miss.

Getting a signature in the clubhouse was easier than getting one in public; I didn't have to fight for my turn with other fans or deal with physical barriers. But there was one intangible obstacle I had to face: the clubhouse is a player's sanctuary, the one place he expects to not be bothered. He assumes he will be able to sit in his underwear and read a book, listen to music, or eat before a game without being harassed, or sulk after a bad game without someone pestering him.

I was able to get autographs that first series from guys like Whitaker, Trammell, and Morris, but I didn't feel comfortable asking Gibson. Had the Tigers won that final game and had he gotten a hit or two, I may have attempted it before he left, but it wasn't worth the risk, especially considering that I would have another chance when they would return to town in a few months. By "risk," I mean that if I were to approach him at the wrong time and he were to say no, I would likely never get his autograph; I wouldn't have the nerve to ask again after being turned down. And, even worse, what if I made him angry enough that he complained to Billy about me bothering him? No autograph was worth my job.

Securing an autograph was about timing, which required some advanced research and effort, such as gauging a player's mood, being aware of how well or poorly he'd been playing as of late, and knowing his general demeanor toward fans. Asking a player as soon as he arrived at the clubhouse each day or minutes before he was about to leave town after the last game of the series were usually the best times. The closer it was to game time, or after a bad game or loss, were the worst times. But every player and situation was different, which was what I had to be wary of.

A lot of my methods for getting an autograph back then can be applied today, in both private and public settings: be polite; treat the player with respect; don't act like it's the player's duty to sign something for you, because it's not; be gracious and say thank you; don't be impatient and annoy the player by yelling his name over and over while he is signing for someone else, as if you will die if he doesn't sign for you, because you won't; don't push other fans out of the way to get what you want; don't be greedy and ask for multiple signatures for yourself, especially when other fans are waiting.

To summarize: don't be a jerk. Most players notice and care about how you behave toward them and the people around you.

One more thing: if you're an adult, act like one. I have no problem with adults getting autographs if it makes them happy, but give kids priority for the simple reason that they are kids. When you're standing among children and you're trying to shove your way past them to get a signature or photo, which I have unfortunately witnessed several times, you look like a fool and much less mature than they do. And if that doesn't bother you, then you probably have much bigger problems that you should address.

The Hated Yankees

I struggled to concentrate in school the day that the Yankees were coming to town. As much as I disliked them as a fan, I was in awe that I was going to meet them. From Babe Ruth to Lou Gehrig to Joe DiMaggio to Mickey Mantle to the stars on the 1986 team, they were the storied franchise.

Just a few players were there when I arrived at the clubhouse, most notably Dave Winfield. At six feet six inches and a muscular 220 pounds, the starting right fielder and future Hall of Famer was imposing and strong, yet affable. He was a standout baseball and basketball player at the University of Minnesota and was selected in the MLB, NBA, ABA, and NFL drafts—and he didn't even play college football. That's how athletic he was. When I walked in, he came over to greet me as if we were old friends. I was stunned.

"Dave Winfield," he said, extending his giant hand toward me.

"Bill. Bill Croyle," I replied, barely able to spit out my name coherently.

"Good to meet you, Bill, Bill Croyle," he said with his trademark smile.

During games throughout the season, the guys in the visitors' bullpen would warm up their right fielder between innings, but not the Yankees.

"Hey, you're going to warm up Dave for us," Yankees' bullpen coach and former Indians' manager Jeff Torborg said to me before the start of the first game.

"I am?" I asked, nervous about this prospect.

"Yep."

"Why me?"

"Because we don't want to," Torborg said.

The Ballboy

I laughed; he didn't. Jeff and the rest of the guys in the pen had no intention of getting out of their chairs until manager Lou Piniella signaled from the dugout for a pitcher to warm up.

Playing catch with a player before a game was fun, but the thought of doing it on the field during a game when everyone was watching was stressful. The distance between the right fielder and where I sat was fairly significant, and I would have no margin for error. Every throw had to be on the money. How embarrassing it would be if I were to launch the ball over Dave's head and had to chase it. But I did as Jeff instructed me to do.

When the Yankees took the field in the bottom of the first inning, I walked up the right field line to get closer to Dave. I stopped in front of the bullpen, about 30 feet away from where the guys were seated. Dave and I started tossing and all was going well when, suddenly, something whizzed past my left ear like a Frisbee and bounced a couple of times along the grass. It was a smashed aluminum can. I turned and looked into the stands.

It's the first inning, I thought. *How could someone already be drunk?*

But it didn't come from the stands. It came from the bullpen where a couple of Yankees, still seated of course, were frantically waving their arms at me to move over so that I wasn't directly in front of them.

"What's wrong?" I shouted.

"We don't want to get hit!" they yelled back.

Well wasn't that nice. The guys who insisted I be the one to play catch with Dave didn't trust that I would catch the ball. Or they didn't trust that Dave could throw the ball to me. Yeah, I'm sure that was it. And couldn't they have used their voices rather than flinging a sharp-edged metal object at my head? Where did they get the can, anyway?

For the record, I didn't miss a single ball Dave threw to me, and all of my throws made it to him. I also retrieved and threw away the aluminum can, because the Yankees certainly weren't going to get up to do it.

As the rest of the players filed into the clubhouse soon after I met Dave, it was a "Who's Who" of baseball: Piniella, Rickey Henderson, Don Mattingly, Ken Griffey Sr., Ron Guidry, Willie Randolph, and Joe Niekro (Phil's brother). As a whole, I could feel the arrogance that I had wondered about them.

"Swagger" may be a fairer term. They were a confident bunch. I wasted no time asking second baseman Willie Randolph for an autograph, but I was met with an unexpected response.

"Who's it for?" he asked.

"For me," I said.

"Come back later." He turned away from me to his locker.

Come back later? Like when? Right before the game? Tomorrow? What does that mean? I was confused, but I said okay and moved on.

I drifted about six lockers over to Rickey Henderson, the star of the team. He still had his reflective shades on and wasn't planning to take them off anytime soon.

"Mr. Henderson, would you please sign this for me?" I usually addressed players as "Mister." It was polite and showed respect. It wasn't until I got to know a player before I called him by his first name.

"Who's it for?" he asked.

Seriously? How about if I say it's for my grandma? Will that make you sign it? I kept those thoughts to myself, of course, but I didn't know what these guys wanted to hear.

"It's for me," I said. I paused for a moment. That was the same answer I gave Willie. I felt like I needed to say something more. "I've been a fan of yours for years," I added. While I was certainly trying to stroke his ego, I wanted to emphasize that it really was for me. It later occurred to me why he and Willie asked me that question. The answer may seem obvious today, though it wasn't so apparent back then.

In the late 1980s, buying and selling sports memorabilia was on the cusp of becoming a booming industry, but it wasn't there yet. Most people, like me, collected memorabilia for themselves, not for profit. But more and more people were turning it into a business. Since the players were the ones doing the signing, I'm sure they recognized this becoming a for-profit trade at a more rapid pace than I could see. Willie and Rickey had no problem signing a ball if it really was for me. But they needed some convincing.

"What's your name?" Rickey asked.

"Bill."

The Ballboy

I'd convinced him.

Rickey took the ball and pen from me and got comfortable in his chair. He took his time writing the "R" and paid careful attention to each stroke of each letter that followed, as if he were being graded on penmanship. The guy was a legend, and he knew it. And people knew that he knew it because of the cockiness he often showed on the field. But he backed it up with his play and hustle. He came across in the media as someone difficult to get along with, but that wasn't my experience. Though he was a temperamental guy, he was approachable if you did it in a respectful way. He and I never had a conversation of any significance, but he signed for me and was polite about it, which left a good impression on me.

At this early stage in my job, many of the superstars and long-time veterans appeared to be the nicest guys. Piniella was very cordial. Mattingly was down-to-earth and treated me like any other guy in the clubhouse. Guidry was nice. That's not to say the lesser-known players weren't nice; most of them were. They just weren't as likely to take the time to talk to me or get to know me, likely because they were focused on their play and staying in the big leagues. The stars were in more of a comfort zone. Yes, some of them had big egos, but not normally too big in the clubhouse to turn me away.

I waited until the next day, after Willie was dressed and packed and ready to get on the bus for the airport, before I approached him again. He looked at me as if he was about to ask again who it was for, but it must have registered with him that he already asked. He signed the ball and told me I was welcome after I thanked him, and off he went to the bus.

The middle game of the series was rained out. The teams split the two games they played, which the Indians followed with a split of two games in Detroit, giving them an overall record of 5-5. Though I only had five games under my belt, I felt like a veteran. Every day was fun, and there was always something to look forward to the next day — like the Orioles, who were coming into town for three games and had a few future Hall of Famers.

Winning Versus Losing

Something that surprised me those first five games that fans couldn't see was how players reacted in the clubhouse after wins and losses.

When a team won, the mood was celebratory. Guys talked loudly, laughed, joked, and enjoyed their dinners. The television was often on with the volume high. Some players and coaches would have a beer, several with an extra dash of salt (I hadn't seen anyone salt their beer prior to this job, but this was a regular practice among many players and coaches). Every win featured a post-game party.

When they lost, clubhouses were dead silent. Some players ate, some didn't. The television was off. The keg went untouched. It was a somber place, not unlike a funeral. When I walked into the Tigers' clubhouse after the second game, their first loss in the series, I thought someone just broke some tragic news to the team.

I don't know what I expected, but I didn't think the moods would be so extreme. It was a long and arduous 162-game season that extended from April through September, or from February through October if you counted spring training and if you made the playoffs. To go from such a high one night after one win to such a low the next night after one loss seemed emotionally draining.

I didn't fully understand yet that for the players, baseball was like any other profession. Whether you're a mechanic, nurse, engineer, accountant, waitress, company president…if you have a good day at work you will be happy, and if you don't, it could negatively affect your mood. Some people feel that guys making a lot of money playing a game should be happy no matter what, but that's not realistic; it's not how we're wired as humans. We can become emotionally distressed when we fail to accomplish something, especially when it involves our livelihood. In terms of baseball, with guys on the bench and in the minor leagues salivating to take a starter's place, errors in the field or struggles at the plate could cost a player his job. Players also have extra incentives to play for, such as post-season berths and future contracts. Those reasons alone make every game count, which is why one loss even early in the season matters to them.

This put me in a precarious position each game. I was quietly rooting for the Indians, but I also didn't like walking into a clubhouse where everyone was feeling lousy, especially when I was wearing the uniform of the team that just beat them. The players and coaches never took out their frustrations on me or on any other clubhouse workers, but it was certainly a more enjoyable environment when they were in a good mood.

I learned over time to adjust to whatever the situation was but to continue doing my job. If the visitors won, I could talk and laugh and go about my business without changing my approach. If it was a loss, I would keep my head down and do my work, staying out of their way when I could and joining them in their silence. As much as I sometimes wanted to call a team meeting and give them my expert analysis of why they lost the game, I didn't think they'd appreciate that.

Earl's Colorful Language

The Orioles had as many popular players as the Yankees in 1986. They were three years removed from winning the World Series over the Philadelphia Phillies and still had a lot of stars: Cal Ripken Jr., Eddie Murray, Fred Lynn, Rick Dempsey, Mike Flanagan, Dennis Martinez, coach Frank Robinson, and manager Earl Weaver. Earl was ejected from nearly 100 games in his career, including a couple of times before games even started. Once, in 1979 in Cleveland, he went on the field with a rule book and tore it into pieces in front of an umpire. Knowing that you might get to witness such antics was worth the price of admission for an Orioles' game.

Terry Pluto, a writer today for the Plain Dealer, covered the Orioles in his early days as a reporter. In a story he wrote after Earl died in 2013, he recalled that Earl used to say to him, "Pluto, I always read your crap when I'm sitting on the toilet…helps loosen things up." He also noted that Earl would string together cuss words in ways that Terry had never heard.

I was fortunate to get my own private showing of one of Earl's magnificent orations before the first game of the series.

When Earl got to the stadium, he seemed to be in a good mood, eager to face the team he'd taken two of three games from in Baltimore a couple of weeks earlier to start the season. But the cold weather completely reversed his disposition. I went down to the dugout with the Gatorade coolers about a half-hour before the game, though hot coffee may have been more appropriate. The temperature had dropped significantly. It was around the mid-50s during the day, but just prior to the 7:35 P.M. start, it plummeted into the 30s. With the wind whipping off Lake Erie, it was easily in the 20s. This was not unusual for Cleveland in mid-April.

The Ballboy

And then the fun really began. It started to snow.

It wasn't sticking to the ground, but it was flurrying hard. With the high winds, it was a faux blizzard, and it sent Earl over the edge. He was sitting on the top of the dugout bench wearing a heavy Orioles jacket with his hands buried in his pockets, silently shivering. It was just the two of us there while the players were in the clubhouse staying warm.

"What the $%^ are we doing out here?" he screamed to nobody in particular before looking at me, his only audience. I figured it was a rhetorical question, so I didn't answer.

"It's $%^&*@# snowing! Can you $%^&*@# see this $%^&*@# snow?" he cried, this time clearly directing the question to me. I felt compelled to answer this time.

"It's coming down pretty hard," I said, stating the obvious while trying very hard not to laugh.

"Do you $%^&*@# think these $%^&*@# umpires can $%^&*@# see that it's $%^&*@# snowing? $%^&! C'mon, call the $%^&*@# game already!"

I'm probably being conservative on the number of expletives he used.

I pivoted and walked toward the other end of the dugout. I had to. It took every ounce of self-control I had to keep my composure. The umpires were still in the umpire room, which was across the field and up the long tunnel next to the Indians' clubhouse. Earl knew they couldn't hear him, even if he had a megaphone. But that didn't stop him from making sure everyone who *could* hear him, which was just me, knew how he felt.

About a minute later, one of the Orioles' coaches came down from the clubhouse.

"Hey," Earl sarcastically shouted to him. "Did you notice it's $%^&*@# snowing out here? And we're about to play a $%^&*@# baseball game!"

The coach turned and looked at me with a huge grin, which I took as a sign that it was okay for me to laugh, so I did. Earl showed no reaction to my reaction. He may have even appreciated it.

That was the Earl Weaver I saw many times on television or read about in the paper, and I was thrilled to have witnessed his ire. He was an extremely nice man off the field. On the field he was all baseball…and nobody knew the game like he did. If he felt that an umpire erred, he made sure the ump and everyone else in the stadium knew it.

To make matters worse for Earl that night, the game wasn't postponed and the Indians won, 7-0. I consciously stayed away from his office after the game, certain that he was pretty $%^&*@# unhappy.

Sucking Up to Eddie

Another volatile Oriole was Eddie Murray. He was already one of the greatest players of all time, in my opinion. On the field and off he was all business and very private. So much so that he had a reputation for not being fan-friendly, and I knew that going into the series.

My first impression of him in the clubhouse was that he wasn't a bad guy, he just wanted to show up to work, do his job, and go home without being bothered or having to talk about it—not much different than some of the hardest workers in any business or industry. He was a leader by example, not with his voice. In fact, when he got to town and a Plain Dealer reporter asked him a simple question about his outstanding start to the season (seven for 12 with two home runs, including a grand slam, and eight RBI), Eddie politely turned down the interview request.

Before the first game of the series, Jim Traber, a rookie for the Orioles who sat a few lockers down from Eddie, asked me if I would get a ball signed by the team for a friend of his. I went around the clubhouse, and everyone I asked obliged. I purposely waited to ask Eddie, figuring if I had other signatures first, he would be more likely to sign. He was standing at his locker adjusting his hat, preparing to head down to the field for batting practice.

"Mr. Murray, can you sign this please?"

"No." He didn't even look at me.

"It's for Mr. Traber," I said nervously. This time he looked directly at me and emphasized his answer.

"No!"

I thought about asking a third time, but I wanted to live long enough to tell this story. As I turned and walked away, Jim emerged from the training room and asked how the signatures were coming along.

"Good, but I didn't get Eddie's," I said.

"Why not?"

"He just doesn't want to sign right now," I said, trying to be nice about it.

Jim smiled.

"Aw, c'mon Eddie, sign the ball!" he bellowed as he walked toward Eddie. Jim's youthful enthusiasm was annoying Eddie to no end. But Jim, a gregarious guy, didn't care. "It's for me. I have people here watching me tonight. C'mon, Eddie, please sign it for me."

Eddie stared crossly at Jim and grunted. He stomped toward me a few steps, grabbed the ball and pen out of my hand, scribbled his name, and pushed it back at me.

"Thanks, Eddie!" Jim exclaimed.

Eddie groaned, grabbed his glove, and left the clubhouse in disgust. *Crap!* I thought. *Eddie's going to hate me for this.* As surly as he was, I wanted his signature for myself because he was such a great player. I also figured that if this was his normal attitude, he probably hadn't signed many autographs relative to other players, possibly making it a rare commodity. The challenge to get it was intriguing, not unlike getting Kirk Gibson's. But I didn't want to keep deferring my autograph attempts until the next time a player was scheduled to come to town. I was determined to get Eddie's before the series ended.

For the rest of that day and for the next two games, I avoided him on and off the field. I made sure I was close enough and available in the clubhouse in case he needed anything, but he didn't summon me. After the final game of the series, I kept an eye on him as I cleaned cleats and did my other tasks. I had a ball and pen in my back pocket, ready to make my move. When he was finally dressed, packed, and ready to head to the bus, I pulled out the ball and pen.

"Mr. Murray, would you mind signing this ball. It's for me. I'd love to have your autograph before you go."

Yeah, major suck up.

Without any attitude, he graciously took the ball and pen, signed it, and handed them back to me.

"Thank you so much," I said.

He gave me an inaudible grumble that I couldn't decipher. It was either "You're welcome" or something that shouldn't be printed, though I'm confident it was the former. Either way, he was nice enough to sign it.

Eddie would club 504 home runs in his career and hit .287 in more than 3,000 games over 21 years. He also played for the Indians in 1995 and was instrumental in them getting to the World Series that season. He was inducted into the Hall of Fame in 2003.

Even if You're Rip Calken Jr., You're Somebody

Whether your name is Cal Ripken Jr. or Rip Calken Jr., when you are in the Major Leagues, you get your own bats with your name engraved in the barrels. When a bat would crack, Carmen and I were usually allowed to take it for ourselves. The only time that wasn't the case was if the crack was small enough that the player would want to tape it and use the bat for batting practice. We would discourage that, of course, because it was not in our best interest.

Carmen and I did not have a system to determine who got what bat. He was the batboy, so I deferred to him on any bats we both wanted, but since we worked together and both worked hard to serve the teams, we kept things as equal as we could and didn't argue. We just divvied them up and were happy with what we got.

During one game that season, Wade Boggs for the Red Sox, who was on his way to his third AL batting title in four years, cracked his bat. I'd heard that it was maybe only the fifth time in his career that he'd done so; that's how good of a hitter he was. Later in that game, when the Red Sox made a pitching change, I met Carmen between home plate and first base to give him the relief pitcher's jacket.

"Wade broke that bat, didn't he?" I asked.

"Yep, and it's mine," Carmen said convincingly, knowing like I did how rare it was. There was going to be no discussion or negotiation.

After the game, as we walked through the concourse to our cars, we ran into Indians' batboy Dan Rocky. Dan also knew Wade cracked the bat, and he offered Carmen a trade.

"Nope," Carmen said.

"How about if I give you…"

"Nope," Carmen repeated, cutting off Dan in mid-sentence.

"Rod Carew?" Dan said. We all went silent.

"Really?" I chimed in. Dan seemed serious. He evidently got a Rod Carew bat the year before when he worked for the visitors. Carew won the AL batting title seven times, something that nobody has done since and likely will never do again. He retired after the 1985 season and was definitely going to be a first-ballot Hall of Famer in five years.

"You have to think about that one," I told Carmen.

He thought about it, but not for long.

"Nope. And we're done talking about it," he said. A Carew bat was an intriguing offer, but because Carmen was the batboy when Wade broke his, I agreed with his choice.

Before the second game of the series with the Orioles, I was in the dugout when Cal Ripken Jr. was taking batting practice. Cal, also a future Hall of Fame player, was known as the "Iron Man" for playing in more consecutive games than anyone in history with 2,632, another record that likely never will be broken. He was a really nice guy who spent some time talking with me and signing a few balls for me that I would give to friends. After he finished taking his swings, he was inspecting the bat on his way back to the dugout. When he reached the dugout, he handed it to me.

"I think it cracked, Bill," he said, "but I don't see it." As he took a seat on the bench, I looked it over. The bat was unique in color. It had a dark brown barrel and a tan handle. Like Cal, I initially didn't see any blemishes. However, as I ran my hand along it during a second inspection, I found the crack. A tiny sliver of wood was slightly protruding from the handle, right where the hands would grip it. He probably didn't feel it because it was so small and he had batting gloves on.

"It did crack," I said. "It's right here in the handle." I was going to walk it over to him to show him, but he nodded his head and took me at my word.

"I thought so," he said. "No big deal."

"Do you want it?" I asked.

"Nah, you can have it," he replied. Upon hearing those magic words, I ran the bat up to my laundry room locker and stuffed it under my duffel bag next to the washing machine before Carmen or anyone else in the clubhouse could claim it. If they had, I'd have fought hard for it given that Cal told me it was mine.

That bat was one of my first. It was always a bonus when I went home with one, no matter whether it belonged to Cal Ripken Jr. or Rip Calken Jr. But it was, of course, much sweeter when it belonged to someone of Cal's stature.

Two Drunk Guys and a Web Gem

During the second game of the Orioles' series, Pat Tabler came up to bat in the later innings. The Indians' first baseman would have a nice 14-year career with five teams, including six of those years with the Tribe, and 1986 would be his best. He would hit .326 for the season, good for fourth in the AL.

As Pat stepped to the plate, I was struggling to stay focused. It was another cold night, the seats were empty, and the Indians were losing. Even John the Cop wasn't there. There were two drunk guys about five rows behind me, but nobody else was in the general vicinity. The announced attendance that night, which was the official paid attendance (not the actual attendance), was 3,004. The stadium was at less than 4 percent capacity. I would generously guess there were about 1,500 people in the stands. It was the kind of game where a fan could yell at a player and everyone in the stadium could hear him. Many of the few season ticket holders stayed home. This was a typical crowd when the Indians stunk and/or it was cold. The Indians didn't stink yet like they normally did by the end of April, but it was darn cold.

One of the pitches by Orioles' hurler Ken Dixon to Pat during that at-bat was a fastball down the heart of the plate. Pat swung and hit the ball harder than it was thrown to him, but he swung late. And a late swing by a right-handed batter meant that I was probably going to get some action.

The ball was lined on a rope. It started slightly to my right, but as is often the case with a hard-hit ball by a right-handed hitter, it was tailing off to my left toward the seats. With barely a second to react, I threw my body against the railing, lunged over as far as I could, and felt and heard the smack of leather against leather. I brought the glove up to my face and opened it, and there was the ball firmly in the webbing. Fundamentally, I did everything right by

65

reacting quickly and not taking my eye off the ball, but I was still as shocked as anyone given how hard it was hit and how much it moved.

The handful of people who witnessed it cheered, one of the few times that they had anything to cheer about that night in a game the Indians would eventually lose, 5-2.

"Nice catch ballboy!" one guy yelled from behind the dugout.

"Put him in the game!" I heard from a voice in the distance.

"Give me the $%^&@#$ ball!" Drunk Guy No. 1 in the seats behind me demanded.

Yeah, I'll get right on that.

He and his buddy were yapping all night, a little more after each beer. They weren't mean, just annoying. They'd probably thrown enough money at the beer vendor to put the vendor's kids through college. Since they were the only two fans in the area, the ball would have been theirs after it ricocheted around the seats, assuming they could fight through their inebriation, stand on their own two feet, and find it, all of which was extremely unlikely.

"We aren't allowed to give balls to fans," I said, using Billy's order as my excuse.

"That's $%^&*@#$!" Drunk Guy No. 1 exclaimed.

"Yeah, that's…that's…" Drunk Guy No. 2 wasn't sure what it was. He quizzically looked to No. 1 for help with completing his sentence, but the help didn't come. They both sat in a stupor.

Of all nights for John the Cop to not be there.

Fortunately for them, they were jolted awake by the beer vendor, who came by and refocused them on what they were best at: ordering a couple of more tall ones. They didn't say anything more about the foul ball, likely forgetting it ever happened.

But here is the best part of the story, from a personal perspective (I won't be hurt if you think the drunk guys were the best part):

As soon as I caught the ball, John Adams emphatically pounded on his drum from the center field bleachers, the uniform sign to every Indians fan that a great play was made. John has attended nearly every home game since 1973. Still today, he sits in the bleachers at Progressive Field and bangs his drum for top plays or to try to start rallies. To hear him pounding it for my catch was an honor that only Indians fans can truly appreciate. I met John seven years later, in October of 1993, at the final game ever played in the old stadium.

"I have to tell you a story," I said. I gave him a brief explanation of what transpired in that game against the Orioles.

"You know what?" John said. "I actually remember that. You reached over the railing and caught it. And it was freezing that night."

I was shocked. He'd been to more than 1,600 games to that point, and he remembered my play?

I met him again about 20 years later at Progressive Field and introduced him to my boys. He no longer remembered me or the play. I didn't expect him to since the Indians had become a formidable team since then and even made a couple of World Series appearances in the 1990s, erasing many of the doldrums from previous years. But he was humbled that a few pounds of the drum still meant so much to me.

Could this Team Actually Be Good?

The Indians took two out of three from the Orioles and went on a nine-game road trip to New York, Texas, and Chicago, where they did the unthinkable after losing the first two games to the Yankees—they won the next seven. They were 14-8, in first place, and coming home for eight games starting May 5 against the defending world champion Kansas City Royals.

Third baseman Brook Jacoby was pounding the ball, hitting .368. Pat Tabler was at .333. Catcher Andy Allanson's average was .375. The starting pitching was doing fairly well, and the bullpen was looking better than a lot of people expected. It was still early, but this was the team's best start in years.

Dealing with something unprecedented, at least in recent memory—a seven game road winning streak and a respectable record this early—the Indians' organization was totally unprepared for the first game against the Royals. They didn't have nearly enough manpower to sell tickets at the ticket windows, forcing the game to start about 15 minutes late. As reported in the Plain Dealer the next day, one scalper said, "I've never done this before at an Indians game." A fan was quoted as saying that he was in line for two and a half hours before he finally gave up. Rocco Scotti, a Cleveland legend who sang the National Anthem that game, said it was nice to sing to people besides "the ushers and the peanut vendors." The announced attendance was more than 27,000, nine times more than any of the games against Baltimore, and most of the ticket sales were walk-ups.

For the fans who didn't get in until late, it was worth the wait. The Indians won a thriller in the tenth inning, 5-4, on Pat Tabler's single that scored Joe Carter. I had never felt such an electric atmosphere at an Indians game.

Several minutes after the winning run scored, the crowd was still cheering, chanting, and insisting that players come out for curtain calls, which a few did.

Because I was in a Tribe uniform, fans at the railing near the dugout were screaming at me to come over to high-five them. When I did, a throng of other fans rushed over to touch me or snap a picture of me…though they mainly wanted to touch me. On this night, the pope couldn't have attracted this much excitement if he'd been standing next to me. It didn't matter that I didn't have a name on the back of my jersey like the players; I was still part of the team, and that's all they cared about. This was the passion Cleveland fans always had. Whether you were the starting pitcher or the ballboy, they wanted in on the excitement. They were expressing exactly what I stated about myself in my essay for the job: they needed to be part of this team at another level.

And, evidently, touching a ballboy was up another level.

The Tribe would play two more games against the Royals and win both convincingly, 6-1 and 7-1, with complete games from knuckleballer Tom Candiotti and lefty Neal Heaton. Their streak was at 10. They attracted nearly 65,000 fans for the weekday series, a significant number for a team that was used to playing in a near-empty stadium. I was so excited, though slightly torn given that the Royals had become my second favorite team.

People Let Me Tell You 'Bout My Best Friend...

The first game against the Royals that the Indians won in extra innings was on a beautiful Monday evening after the Tribe had been gone for 10 days. I was excited to get back to work. As soon as school ended I went straight to the stadium, hauled everything into the dugout myself before Carmen got there, and returned to the clubhouse to gawk at the players: Bret Saberhagen, George Brett, Frank White, Willie Wilson, Hal McRae, Steve Balboni, Lonnie Smith, Jim Sundberg, Dan Quisenberry. These were the defending world champions.

When they started to head down for batting practice, I followed and sprinted to the outfield to shag fly balls. This was one of my favorite times of each day. It wasn't a job that was required, but it was much appreciated by the teams. Pitchers and other players who weren't taking batting practice would normally stand in the outfield in small groups and catch fly balls off the bats of hitters, assuming the balls came right to them; they weren't about to exert any energy to chase them. It was more a time for them to socialize with each other and the fans. I, on the other hand, found it exhilarating to sprint across the outfield after any ball hit by a Major Leaguer.

As I stood alone in center field waiting for the next batter to step in, I noticed one of the Royals who'd just come out of the dugout walking in my direction. Since nobody was standing near me, I figured he would veer toward his teammates in left or right field. But he didn't. As he got closer, I could see that he was wearing No. 5. Every baseball fan in the world knew who that was. I waited for him to take a detour, but it was becoming apparent that I was his destination. I'm not embarrassed to say that my heart skipped a few beats.

"Hey, how are ya?" he said as he approached and extended his hand. "I'm George Brett."

I nervously laughed as I shook his hand.

"Yes, I know who you are," I said. "I'm Bill Croyle."

"Bill, it's nice to meet you. What do you do for the Indians?"

"I'm the ballboy down the right field line, and I work in your clubhouse."

"Cool! How did you get that job?"

For the next 30 minutes we talked, and talked, and talked. He asked me about school, family, work, anything he could think of. I got more comfortable as the conversation progressed, but I continually heard my voice in my head reminding me, *This is George Brett! Don't say something stupid, you dumb#$%!* Or maybe it was Billy's voice I heard. Either way, I chose my words carefully.

George was one of the game's greatest hitters. He would retire a 13-time All-Star, accumulate more than 3,000 hits, and end his career with a batting average of .305. In 1980, he finished the season with an astonishing .390 average. His pursuit that year to become the first person to hit .400 since Ted Williams had done it in 1941 captivated the nation.

A lot of players on different teams struck up conversations with me throughout the year, but none took as much time or were as present in the moment as George. It was absolutely surreal, just the two of us on a Major League field having a heart-to-heart talk. And he seemed to be enjoying it as much as I was.

"Have you met Dick Howser yet?" he asked. Dick was the Royals' manager.

"Not yet," I said.

"C'mon. I want you to meet him."

Sometimes during batting practice, Carmen and I would take turns standing behind second base as the cutoff man and catch any balls that outfielders retrieved. We'd drop the balls into a bag and run the bag to the batting practice pitcher when he needed them. As George and I headed toward the dugout to meet Dick, Carmen, who was the cutoff guy for all of batting practice so far, called me to relieve him.

"I can't. I have to go with George," I yelled.

"What? C'mon! I've been doing this the whole time!"

He was right. It was my turn. But that wasn't happening.

"Sorry," I said, shrugging my shoulders and pointing to George.

"Do you have to go over there?" George asked me.

"Nope, we're good," I said. Carmen wasn't happy based on the finger he showed me, but no way was this encounter going to end until George decided it was time.

While George had to have known that he was giving me an incredible story to tell, he didn't make me feel that that was why he approached me. It was more like he decided that he was going to make himself a new friend that day, and I was it. The only thing missing as we walked together toward the dugout was a boom box on my shoulder playing *Best Friend*, the theme song from the early '70s television show *The Courtship of Eddie's Father* (if you're too young, and if you'd like a good laugh, find the song on YouTube and listen to it as you picture George and me walking across the field together).

When we reached the dugout, he introduced me to Dick and told him everything he learned about me over the past half hour. I was stunned at the information George retained, more proof of how genuine of a person he was. When George was finished, Dick asked me a few more questions about myself. I was in awe at what was transpiring.

Are all of the guys on the team like this? I wondered.

They were. Wilson, White, Balboni—every single player on that roster treated me like I was one of them.

Before the third game, I ran to center field again hoping that George would soon join me. He didn't. But Dan Quisenberry did. He was the team's submarine-style pitcher, one of the best relievers in the game. I guess you could say he made a relief appearance for George to keep me entertained.

"Hi, I'm Dan," he said as he shook my hand.

"I know," I said. "I'm Bill Croyle." It was déjà vu, though this time with Dan. For the rest of batting practice, Dan and I talked about my future goals, and he even offered me some advice. Toward the end of our conversation, George meandered over. Dan tried to introduce him to me.

"Oh, I know Bill already," George said.

Unreal.

In 1987 and 1998, respectively, Dick Howser and Dan Quisenberry passed away, both from brain cancer. I teared up when I read about their deaths, and my emotions are still stirred when I think about them. Imagine, if these men were that nice to a stranger like me, what they must have been like as sons, husbands, fathers, and friends. Their presence and kindness made a lasting impression on me, even though our time together was brief.

Mounds of Shaving Cream

After the Royals were swept out of town, the Indians played three games at home against the Chicago White Sox and two with the Rangers. Unfortunately, the Tribe lost four of those five games, including all three to the White Sox in bizarre fashion.

The Friday night game drew nearly 50,000 fans, but the energy wasn't enough to propel the Indians to victory. The White Sox won, 4-3, when they scored three runs in the ninth inning off the bullpen after Phil Niekro pitched seven solid innings. Saturday was eerily similar. The Sox won, 4-0, in 11 innings after Indians' starting pitcher Ken Schrom threw 10 scoreless innings. Again, the bullpen. Chicago scored two in the eighth on Sunday for another one-run win. Instead of a 13-game winning streak, we were on a three-game losing streak, two games behind the first-place Red Sox and a game behind the second-place Yankees.

Despite sweeping the Indians, the White Sox were not very good that year. Their manager when they came to town was Tony La Russa, who would later be fired and come back to Cleveland in September as the manager of the A's. The Sox had a mix of young guys like John Cangelosi and Ozzie Guillen, and future Hall of Famers Harold Baines and Carlton Fisk.

Carlton's locker was the first one on the left when I entered the clubhouse, and I instantly recognized him. He was a big guy with broad shoulders, very nice and approachable. Carlton hit the game-winning home run for the Red Sox against the Reds in game six of the 1975 World Series to force a game seven. You may have seen that famous video of him waving his arms, trying to will the ball fair over the Green Monster at Fenway Park. It was such an iconic moment in baseball history. To be this close to the person responsible for it was astounding.

Beyond recognizing Carlton right away, my most glaring memory of the White Sox is their pranks. Well, prank—the same one over and over again, and it never got old. Maybe because they struggled to win games, it was a way to absorb the losing and stay loose during the season. Or, maybe they struggled to win games because they were too focused on their mischievous behavior. Whatever the case, they were fun to be around.

Their running joke was to squirt shaving cream discreetly on top of each other's hats. It was so simple, yet hilarious. A player would sneak up behind another, squirt a pile on top of his hat, and let him wander wherever he so desired without him knowing what rested above. It was almost an art form, trying to put on as much as possible without it falling off and without being caught. Some guys ran onto the field during batting practice topped with it and were oblivious until they returned to the dugout to bat. I don't recall who the ringleader was, but by the end of the series so many players were involved that it was easier to count who wasn't in on it. You had to know who was behind you at all times or you would likely fall victim.

In the clubhouse prior to the second game I was talking to Carmen, who earlier pompously proclaimed that no player would be able to pull this stunt on him. As he and I were talking, one of the players sneaked behind him with a fresh can and motioned me to keep my conversation with Carmen going.

"Did you take the Gatorade down?" I asked Carmen.

"Yeah, I told you that already," he said.

"And I assume the bats and helmets are all set up?"

Carmen looked at me like I was a complete idiot. Meanwhile, the player carefully squirted a fresh mound onto Carmen's cap.

"Of course they're set up!"

"Everything?"

"No, I took out four bats and two helmets. The rest of the players can get their own stuff!"

His sarcasm was a clear signal that I was annoying him.

The player added a decent-sized second dollop, but he signaled me to keep talking. I think he wanted to try to empty the can. This was risky. I was running out of material.

"So, what else needs to go down?"

"Everything is down there!" Carmen snapped. "I told you that!"

"Why are you getting so mad?" I asked.

"Why are you asking me such stupid questions?"

"Sorry, man, just making sure we're set for the game."

Our brief argument was well worth it. As I walked away, Carmen had a heaping glob of shaving cream on his hat that rivaled the snow caps atop the Rocky Mountains. I thought it was going to topple over, but it hung on. The player did a masterful job. Carmen walked for a good half hour around the clubhouse, in the dugout, and, best of all, around the on-deck circle for fans to see before the game. I walked to the top of the dugout steps and put my finger over my lips, signaling the fans to not say anything. Not only did they not tell him, a few of them snapped pictures. It's a shame social media wasn't a thing yet.

I thought that I made it through the weekend unscathed, but in the dugout just before the third game, as I was about to run onto the field to shag fly balls, I saw Carmen glance at me with a quick smirk. And thank goodness he did. We were all so much on edge about getting pranked, that that smirk was all it took. I yanked off the hat and found a mound that could have covered my face for a week's worth of shaves. We were the only two in the dugout, so they obviously got me in the clubhouse. For as vigilant as I was, I was shocked that they pulled it off, but they were *that* good.

I still have my hat that fell victim to Chicago's shaving cream shenanigans, and it still has a tiny faded white stain on it. While I'm not encouraging you to ruin someone's hat, if you're bored one day and want to liven things up…

The Grip

The Indians split their two games with the Rangers, dropping the Tribe into third place, but they were still only two games out of the top spot. The first game was an unconventional 19-2 loss in which 18 of the Rangers' runs were scored in the last four innings. Reliever Jim Kern gave up seven earned runs on six hits and three walks in one and one-third of an inning. As he exited the field, a fan threw a glass beer bottle in Jim's direction that barely missed him. It was a whole seven days since the Kansas City game when more than 27,000 fans didn't want to go home after the victory. Now they were launching lethal objects at the players.

The next night, the Indians would snap their four-game losing streak with a 3-2 win in 10 innings. Fans drank their beer, placed the bottles in the proper receptacles, and were happy once again.

The highlight for me during the brief series was meeting Rangers' pitcher Charlie Hough. Charlie was playing for the Los Angeles Dodgers when he gave up Reggie Jackson's third home run in game six of the 1977 World Series at Yankee Stadium to seal the championship for New York, an unforgettable moment in baseball history. Like meeting Carlton Fisk the previous series, to be able to meet the player behind such a classic moment brought that history to life.

Charlie was famous for his knuckleball. In fact, in the clubhouse before the 19-2 game, I saw a journalist ask Charlie to sign a ball and trace the grip of his knuckleball on it. I thought that would have been something that Charlie would have kept secret, but he was more than happy to do it. Realizing what a unique souvenir that would be, I had to get one for myself. After the game, I approached him.

"Well, I just showered," Charlie said, not looking too thrilled about potentially getting pen on his clean hand.

"I can ask you again tomorrow," I replied.

"Nah, it's okay," he said. "I'll just do it now."

Like Rickey Henderson signed his autograph with such precision, Charlie did the same—though he was probably more concerned about not getting ink on himself. He methodically traced his grip, putting small hash marks where he digs the fingernails of his index and middle fingers into the ball, and outlining where his thumb and other two fingers are positioned. He then signed it to me. I've been able to throw his knuckleball a few times, though not very effectively. Any youngster with large hands who can learn how to throw it would probably be pretty tough to hit.

The Charlie Hough ball ranks as one of my favorite pieces of memorabilia. He would play for 25 years, finish with an even record of 216 wins and 216 losses, and be inducted into the Rangers' Hall of Fame.

Standing Up to a Bully

Mitch Williams was a six-foot four-inch, 205-pound hard-throwing lefthanded rookie for the Rangers in 1986. He was a decent pitcher who in 1993 would help lead the Phillies to the World Series. Nicknamed "Wild Thing" after the Charlie Sheen character in the movie *Major League,* he did have some control issues. In 691.1 innings pitched (nearly all in relief) during his 11-year career, Mitch walked 544 batters, threw 44 wild pitches, plunked 52 hitters, and was called for 24 balks.

I knew it was commonplace for rookies in many professional sports to be hazed by their teammates, and while the Rangers were in Cleveland, I witnessed Mitch go through it. Before the first game, when he came out of the training room and went to his locker, he found that someone meddled with his personal belongings. I don't know what they did, nor do I recall which teammate was responsible. Mitch, however, immediately knew who it was, because it wasn't the first time. He was fed up with it and walked over to the guy, who was standing in the middle of the clubhouse seemingly waiting for Mitch's reaction.

"Tell me," Mitch said loudly, standing face to face with the culprit, "why do you always mess with my stuff? Why is it always me? Why do you do it?"

His teammate laughed but didn't respond.

"I want an answer!" Mitch demanded. The guy continued to laugh but struggled to keep eye contact with Mitch. Everyone in the clubhouse watched in silence.

"Every trip we're on you mess with my stuff," Mitch said. "I want to know why you do it. Why me? What joy do you get from it?"

81

The player still didn't speak, and his laugh was now barely a grin; he was clearly uncomfortable. I was witnessing a bully get a taste of his own medicine. The player turned and walked to his locker, so Mitch followed him. I didn't sense that Mitch was going to start a physical fight. If he had, I think everyone, including that player, knew that Mitch would have pounded him. It also wouldn't have been a smart thing to do to a teammate, especially as an unproven rookie. Mitch simply wanted the harassment to end.

When they were both at the player's locker, the player sat down...so Mitch pulled up the chair from the locker next to him and sat down, too. That's when the player gave in and acknowledged how upset Mitch was by saying he would stop bothering him. But Mitch continued to hammer him.

"Just tell me *why* you do it," Mitch insisted. The player kept his head down, mouth shut, and started to get dressed for the game. Mitch, knowing that he made his point and that he wasn't going to get an answer, finally backed off and returned to his own locker.

My guess is that that guy didn't give Mitch any more trouble the rest of the season.

Garbage Picking

Rangers' pitcher Mike Mason would play for eight years and end his career with 29 wins and 39 losses, though he would finish the 1986 season with a decent 7-3 record. I can't recall if I knew who Mike was before he came to town. He certainly was not a guy on my list of Rangers I had to meet, like Hough, Ruben Sierra, Toby Harrah, or Pete Incaviglia.

Yet I still have his grimy old hat.

I was walking through the clubhouse when I passed the garbage can in the middle of the room. It was nearly full, and right on top was a Rangers hat. I thought it was knocked accidentally into the can off the nearby table, so I pulled it out. It had Mason's No. 16 written in black marker underneath the bill. The hat was filthy with sweat stains and black goo around the inside brim, probably from the eye black that athletes rub under their eyes to reduce the glare from the sun. One of the clubhouse attendants was walking by as I pulled it out.

"What are you doing?" he asked.

"Is this supposed to be in here?"

"Yeah, he got a new hat today. Throw that away."

I looked over at Mike's locker. He already went down to the field.

"So...can I have this one?" I asked.

"No."

"Why not?"

"Because it's gross!" the attendant said.

"But if Mike doesn't want it, why can't I have it?"

"It's disgusting!"

"But it's a Major League player's hat," I persisted.

I wasn't going to let this go unless I was given a good reason why I couldn't have it.

"You know what? Do whatever you want," he said.

Argument over. I took the hat.

That incident reminds me today of an episode of *Seinfeld* (I still claim that we're all living in a *Seinfeld* episode) when George pulled a pastry out of a garbage can and bit into it. After being caught, he tried every possible way to justify what he did. When Jerry asked him if it was in the cylinder of the garbage can, as if that would matter, George vehemently replied, "Above the rim!" In the same way, I'm almost certain the top of Mike's cap was above the rim. Even if it wasn't, this was a Major League hat worn by a Major League player. What more justification did I need for pulling it from the trash?

Few baseball fans, outside of die-hard Rangers fans, probably have any recollection of Mike. However, I did read that he continued his career as a pitching coach in the Chicago Cubs' minor league system. Given that they finally won the World Series in 2016, maybe he had a hand in developing their talent. Even if he didn't, I'm still glad I went garbage picking that day. It's the only game-worn hat, other than my own, that I would take home that season.

A Post-Brawl Meeting of the Minds

Following the series with the Rangers, the Indians left for nine games against Kansas City, Toronto, and Milwaukee, and it was an ugly start. They lost both games to the Royals and three of four to the Blue Jays. Fortunately, they were able to salvage two out of three from the Brewers. They left Milwaukee with a record of 21-18 and were in fourth place, five games out of first behind Boston. This was a significant accomplishment for a team that won just 60 games the year before and was normally out of the pennant race at this point in late May. Just 39 games in, they were already six games ahead of their 1985 pace.

They returned home for nine games starting Memorial Day weekend, three each against Toronto, Boston, and Milwaukee. So many memories with players would come out of the Boston and Milwaukee games, which is likely why I don't recall much about the series with the Blue Jays outside of an autographed ball, a broken bat, and a brawl.

The first game against the Jays was on a Friday night and attracted 61,340 fans. The Indians won, 3-1, and it took barely more than two hours to play. The Tribe would lose the next two, 9-6 and 8-1.

The Blue Jays won the division the previous season and had a powerful lineup that included Jesse Barfield, George Bell, Lloyd Moseby, Willie Upshaw, and Cliff Johnson. Barfield, Bell, and Moseby comprised one of the best outfields baseball had seen in a long time, both defensively and offensively, and I made sure to get a ball autographed by the three of them.

I was also fortunate to get one of George Bell's broken bats. George would hit 265 home runs in a 12-year career, including 31 in 1986 (two in that series against the Tribe) and 47 the next year. Of all the broken bats I took home that season, his was the biggest piece of lumber. How he was able to get it

85

around so quickly on a fastball was a testament to how strong he was and how quick his reflexes were.

The most memorable event of that series, a first for me to witness while being on the field, was a benches-clearing brawl. It was during the second game and involved Blue Jays' pitcher Dave Stieb and Indians' left fielder Mel Hall. Stieb was one of the league's top pitchers for several seasons, including 14 wins and a 2.48 earned run average (ERA) the previous year. Mel was an aggressive guy with power who never shied away from a confrontation.

In the bottom of the second inning during a scoreless game, Dave drilled Mel with a pitch. The split second he was hit, Mel dropped his bat and charged the mound. The brawl was on. Both dugouts and bullpens emptied.

With my adrenaline skyrocketing as the Blue Jays' bullpen guys charged past me like a herd of thoroughbreds, I can't tell you how much I wanted to race in with them and join the melee. I wasn't a fighter at all, but I knew baseball fights weren't really fights. They were 50 or 60 players and coaches doing some pushing and shoving and talking and getting acquainted with one another while only a couple of guys tried to throw punches. After the game, Pat Tabler called it "…your basic baseball brawl. Everybody was just standing around." I wouldn't have gotten hurt, but I probably would have lost my job, so I stayed in my chair.

I don't believe Dave hit Mel on purpose. I hadn't heard of any bad blood between the players or teams, and nobody was hit the night before. Pat Tabler was hit by Dave in a game the previous week in Toronto, and Mel went four for four against him one game in that same series; that could have been the catalyst, but I don't know. After the game, Dave told the media that he was trying to pitch Mel inside, not hit him. The umpires didn't think his bean ball was intentional, because Mel was the only person ejected. Dave came out of the fight physically unscathed, but it messed him up mentally.

After the brawl ended and the game resumed, Otis Nixon came in to pinch run for Mel, and the Indians proceeded to erupt for four runs in the inning. When the inning was finished and the Indians were warming up in the field, I saw Carmen running toward me from the dugout. I got up and met him near first base. He looked fired up.

"What's up?" I asked.

"You should see Stieb!" he said.

"What's he doing?"

"He's sitting at the end of the dugout shaking."

"Really?" I had no idea how players reacted in the dugout after a brawl.

"Yeah, Mel really rattled him," Carmen said.

The Indians' pitcher was warmed up and the batter was making his way to the plate, and there we were chatting. He still didn't tell me why he came over. The only time the two of us ever met during a game was when a pitcher was called in from the bullpen and I had to bring his jacket to Carmen. Carmen was a bit eccentric, but was he crazy enough to leave his post in the dugout and run across the field mid-game just to tell me how shaken up Dave was?

"Yeah, that's all," he said as he backpedaled toward the dugout with a grin. "Hey, I had to tell somebody!"

I think we were both hoping that there would be more batters hit just to see how much the animosity would escalate, but players from both teams behaved themselves for the rest of the game.

The Lovely Vanna White

The Red Sox came in for three games with a 28-14 record and still in first place, six games ahead of the Indians. Many baseball prognosticators expected them to be very good that year, and the Sox were backing it up early. With a lineup that included Wade Boggs, Bill Buckner, Jim Rice, Dwight Evans, and Marty Barrett, they were a tough offense to contain. Their pitchers were solid, too, with a hidden gem among the starters named Roger Clemens.

Roger entered the league with huge fanfare out of the University of Texas when he was 21 years old. He went 9-4 his first season and 7-5 his second year. Though he was the team's No. 4 starter his third year in 1986 behind Bruce Hurst, Dennis "Oil Can" Boyd, and Al Nipper, many thought it might be his breakout year...and it was.

When Boston arrived in Cleveland, Roger was 8-0. I went directly to his locker when I got to the stadium, excited to meet him, but he was already down at the field. I wasted no time changing into my uniform and hustling down to the dugout where I encountered a line of journalists and photographers, shoulder to shoulder, at the top of the steps. I maneuvered my way around them...and there he was.

Roger was about six feet four inches tall and 200 pounds. He looked even larger than that, probably because it was almost June and he was still undefeated. He was doing nothing more than jogging in foul territory between third base and home plate, but the media couldn't get enough of it. Photographers' cameras clicked in rapid fire like machine guns while writers and reporters scribbled notes and watched in awe, like they were in the presence of a godlike figure.

The Ballboy

There was only one other person I saw that season who was treated at an Indians' game with such reverence: the lovely Vanna White.

Vanna, who has turned letters on the game show *Wheel of Fortune* since 1982, was in town for a game a couple of weeks earlier to promote the show, which was the highest-rated game show in television history. She and Pat Sajak, the show's host, were there to throw out the first pitch, though Pat didn't seem to be getting quite the attention that the 29-year-old Vanna was receiving from the players and the predominantly male press. Go figure.

With the grounds crew doing last-minute touch-ups to the infield before the game, I looked from the top step of the visitors' dugout and saw Vanna in the Indians' dugout across the way. I usually hung in the visitors' dugout until I had to take my seat down the right field line, but on this day, with Vanna in one dugout and no Vanna in the other dugout, why was I in the no-Vanna dugout? I grabbed my glove and headed to the other side.

Pat Sajak was standing on the field speaking with one of the team's front office personnel. Vanna was sitting in the middle of the dugout bench talking to a couple of players. I took a seat toward the end of the bench on the side where the players were sitting, trying not to make it too obvious that I was there just to see her. After a minute or so, the players between us got up to do some stretching on the field.

It left Vanna and me all alone.

That's when it hit me that this was my big chance. For what, I had no idea. But when you're alone with Vanna White and nothing but 10 feet of bench between you, you don't not do *something!*

With my heart racing, I surreptitiously turned my head toward her. Decked out in an Indians jersey the team gave her, she was looking straight ahead at the field while sitting with prefect posture and her hands folded in her lap. I tried to will myself to say hi, but I couldn't. My shyness was in high gear. I looked away from her and toward the field, took a deep breath, and turned my head again.

Yep, she was still there.

You idiot! I screamed to myself. *Say hi to her! Say it! Say it! Sayyyyy iiiiit!* Evidently, Sam Kinison was now in my head.

I looked toward the field once more, took another deep breath, and turned my head for the third time…

Gulp.

Vanna was staring right at me. And smiling. Smiling like she'd just spotted her best friend. I was terrified, but in a good way, and I instinctively smiled back. This moment was the foreplay of a magical and exhilarating conversation that I haven't forgotten, one I'm sure she too still has stored in her memory.

"Hi," I said nervously.

"Hi!" she replied enthusiastically, as one would expect from Vanna.

For me to muster the courage to spit out two full letters, both a consonant *and* a vowel, was remarkable. I'm sure I left her longing for more, like maybe a conjunction or compound word, but the front office person talking to Pat summoned Vanna to come out to get ready to throw the first pitch. Our time together ended. Too soon. *Way* too soon.

Back to Roger…

He didn't pitch against the Indians that series, but the Red Sox didn't need him. They would sweep the three games, dropping the Indians nine games back. Fortunately, the Red Sox would be back in August, possibly giving me another chance to see Roger pitch.

Okay, back to Vanna …

In 1990, my fiancée and I would take a vacation to Southern California where we would see a taping of *Wheel of Fortune*. Unfortunately, probably because of the lighting or something, Vanna did not recognize me in the audience. I was sad that we couldn't speak again and rekindle that special moment we had together in the dugout four years earlier, but I'm grateful that I—I mean "we"—will forever have that scintillating two-word conversation in our hearts.

The Fog Game

The second game of the series against Boston was on a Tuesday evening and would go down in history as "The Fog Game." Mother Nature normally has a good sense of humor in Cleveland considering all of the different weather she throws at the city, though the Indians didn't find this latest gag very funny.

It started as a quiet evening with an announced attendance of 6,661. The air was warm, around 70 degrees, and the humidity was very high. As the game progressed, fog gradually rolled in from beyond center field off the lake. By the third inning it was a light haze. By about the bottom of the fourth, right fielder Dwight Evans was shouting to his teammates in the bullpen that the ball was getting difficult to see. In the last of the fifth inning, the guys in the bullpen were shouting to Dwight that *he* was getting difficult to see.

In the bottom of the sixth, nearly two hours into the game, the fog was so thick that crew chief umpire Larry Barnett stopped play. The Indians had Tony Bernazard on first base and nobody out; the Red Sox were clinging to a 2-0 lead. That's when things started to heat up.

Not convinced that it was too difficult to see, Indians' manager Pat Corrales jogged to right field near Dwight at the start of the delay. Boston manager John McNamara followed. Then center fielder Tony Armas and left fielder Jim Rice drifted over. A couple of umpires went out there, too. Everybody was being civil, but I was close enough to hear some polite arguing amongst them that went something like this:

"I can see."

"I can't see at all."

"How can you not see if I can see?"

"There's no way that you can see."

"Don't tell me what I can or can't see!"

With this argument spinning in circles, and to try to prove that the ball could be seen, Indians' hitting coach Bobby Bonds stood near first base and hit a fly ball to Dwight. He caught it, but he claimed he could see it only because it hit the perfect spot in the lights. So, Bobby hit another one. This time Dwight didn't move as the ball soared over the fence, sparking a cheer for Bobby from the crowd.

"I didn't see it," Dwight said.

"I did!" Pat Corrales exclaimed.

One of the umpires said he saw it leave the bat but didn't see it leave the yard. I had the same perspective as that umpire. I initially saw it, but I didn't see it land. I only knew it landed because what goes up must come down, and I knew it went over the fence because of the crowd's reaction.

After a few more minutes of discussion among the men, and after Larry talked it over with his fellow umpires, the game resumed. I was glad that they were playing; it would give the Indians a chance to come back. But I was surprised given the low visibility.

Over the next 15 minutes, the fog thickened. During that time, Julio Franco singled, Joe Carter flew out, and Mel Hall hit a long drive to center that Tony Armas chased down and caught near the wall. So they *could* see. But now with two outs, runners on first and second, and the go-ahead run in Pat Tabler coming to bat, Dwight jogged to the infield and told Larry that the visibility was dangerously low. Larry stopped the game again, and Pat Corrales lost it. He furiously charged out of the dugout and had to be separated from Larry by another umpire, but Larry wasn't swayed. The game was delayed again.

It was about 9:45 P.M. at the start of the second delay, and the stadium was eerily quiet. There were no players on the field. Many frustrated fans left. The scoreboard was swallowed by the fog. A colony of bats swooped and squeaked overhead. About the only thing missing was the grim reaper, and the only thing keeping us grounded in reality was the sound of the beer vendors' voices trying to sell their stock.

Roughly 45 minutes into the delay and bored out of his mind, one of the Red Sox pitchers in the bullpen set a baseball on the grass and smacked it into the outfield fog, using his bat like a golf club. As he sauntered into the haze to find the ball, he completely disappeared and would never return to the pen.

A few minutes later, now a little after 10:30 P.M., a fan about my age came down to the railing and asked if I could get her a player's autograph, pointing at the Red Sox bullpen.

"I can't do that," I said.

"Why not?"

"Because players can't sign during games."

"Why not?"

"Because they aren't allowed."

"But the game isn't going on."

"But we are still technically in the midst of the game."

"All I want is one," she pleaded. "The Indians are my favorite team."

I stayed silent for a moment to let her last statement soak into her noggin, to see if she was serious. She was.

"Those aren't the Indians," I said. "Those are the Red Sox."

"No they're not."

"Yes they are."

"No they're not."

"Can you read the name on their uniforms?" I asked in an irritated tone. I wasn't trying to be mean or embarrass her, but why was this conversation even happening? After staring at the players for a few seconds through the fog, she turned and left in a huff without saying another word.

Just a few minutes later, as if one insane fan was passing the baton to the next, a guy in a Red Sox cap came down to the railing to ask me to ask the Red Sox bullpen guys if they ever heard of Pumpsie Green. Pumpsie was the first black Red Sox player, debuting in 1959. I presumed most Red Sox fans and personnel knew that.

"I'm sure the players know who he is," I said.

"Can you just ask?"

"Sir…"

"Please? C'mon," he begged.

None of this was in my job description. Or maybe it was, since I was never provided an official job description. I went to the bullpen and reluctantly asked. As I expected, the guys were insulted that I would bring such a question to them.

"They know who he is," I told the gentleman when I returned. "He was the first black player to play for the Red Sox."

"I figured," he said proudly.

"You figured he was the first black player or you figured that they knew?"

"Oh, I knew who he was."

"Then why did you have me ask them?"

"I wanted to see if they knew. I used to work in the Red Sox organization."

"You did? Doing what?"

He stopped making eye contact with me.

"It was years ago," he said, not answering my question.

We both stood there, me staring at him in disbelief for wasting my time, and him gazing into the distance as if he were posing for a dramatic photo after proving to himself whatever it was that he just proved to himself. Of course, there was nothing to see in the distance because of the fog, so I don't know what he was looking at.

This was what the night had become. We'd gone from watching a good baseball game between two solid teams to witnessing a lot of strange, inexplicable events and people. Part of the problem was that this delay was unprecedented. During a rain delay, fans would take cover in the concourse or snuggle under umbrellas or raincoats. In a fog delay in warm weather, people didn't know what to do with themselves. So they drank or harassed the ballboy.

The umpires finally called the game at about 11:30 P.M. Five and two-thirds innings and a 2-0 Red Sox win, roughly four hours after the first pitch. During postgame interviews, Dwight said, "I'm not going to say I can see the ball when I can't." Pat Corrales responded by saying that Dwight "didn't want to play." It was nothing more than an extension of the silly conversation I'd overheard them having in right field during the first delay.

On the bright side, when I returned to the clubhouse, I think I may have spotted the bullpen pitcher who wandered into the fog to golf. But I will never be certain.

I Disappointed Dwight

When the Red Sox first arrived in town, Dwight Evans called me over to his locker. Dwight already cemented himself as a Boston legend. He broke in with the Red Sox at the age of 20 in 1972 when he played in 18 games. He was a regular by 1973, and he hit at least 22 home runs each year since 1981. He was putting up solid numbers again in 1986, and he would have his best year across the board in 1987.

I rushed to his locker like a dog called to get a treat. Anytime a player summoned me, I knew it probably meant that he had a task for me, which would give me a chance to get to know him and likely give me a good story to tell.

"What's your name?" he asked politely.

"Bill," I said.

"Bill," Dwight replied, "do you know who Pumpsie Green was?"

I'm kidding.

He handed me a couple of baseballs and asked me to get them signed by all of the players.

"I don't need them right away," he said. "Just sometime before we leave is fine."

This should have been a simple task. I did it for Jim Traber when the Orioles came to town and for a few other players since. But it wasn't.

Though I had my usual jobs to do before and after games, they rarely prevented me from taking on extra tasks such as Dwight's. However, many of the Red Sox players, for whatever reason, went down to the field far earlier than previous teams had, and we were not allowed to ask players for autographs when they were in the dugout or on the field, even if the signatures were for another player. (I mentioned that Clemens was already on the field when I got to the stadium for that first game; seldom were players ever down there before I arrived, but many Red Sox were. That could be why they were in first place.)

I still didn't think this would be a huge problem; I could get players to sign after games. And I did just that after the first game, and I planned to do it again after the second…but the fog rolled in. It was after midnight when the players were done showering and eating, and they wanted to get back to their hotel.

I did the best I could those first two days and got most of the signatures, but I was missing some. Realizing that I was running out of time, I gave them to one of the clubhouse workers before the third game and asked him if he could get the rest while I took care of my other tasks.

"Sure, no problem," he said.

But he didn't. He couldn't, for the same reason that I couldn't. He was able to get a couple more, but some players weren't available when he was available. After the game I returned the balls to Dwight.

"I didn't have time to get everybody, so I gave them to another worker who got a couple more. We're only missing a few," I said, figuring he'd be okay with that or he could get those last few himself.

"What do you mean you gave the balls to another worker?" he asked. His inquiry caught me off guard.

"I had to get to the field to get some things done," I said, "so I asked one of the other clubhouse guys to get what he could for me."

"But Bill, I asked *you* to get them."

He truly didn't look happy.

"I know you did," I replied. "I thought I would do what I could to get you as many signatures as possible, which is why I asked the other guy to help me."

To me, it was about getting him the signatures. To him, it seemed to be about *me* getting him the signatures.

"Okay," he said, still visibly disappointed.

"I'm really sorry about that," I said sincerely as I walked away.

I Disappointed Dwight

Maybe Dwight believed that when you accept a task, you should do the best that you can to complete it yourself and not pass it on to someone else. I believed that when you accept a task, you do whatever it takes to get it completed, even if it means asking someone for help. Neither of us was wrong, we just weren't on the same page as to what the priority was. A simple miscommunication.

I also have wondered if, from his perspective, it was a situation somewhat similar to the one with George Brett…one in which Dwight picked me as "his guy" for those few days. But, in this case, dumb#$% me went and picked another guy to help me be Dwight's guy. Whatever the reason for his reaction, I felt bad for not coming through the way he wanted me to.

The story does have a nice ending, though. As Dwight was leaving the clubhouse for the bus to go to the airport, he tipped me $10. Billy received tips all the time from nearly every player; it was proper etiquette to tip the clubhouse manager. But Carmen and I rarely received them. The one from Dwight was my first. I guess everything was cool between us. Tip or no tip, he would rank among the nicest guys I would meet that season, and he became one of my favorite players.

"Jim Rice Still Owes Us Money"

Indians fans despised the Red Sox almost as much as the Yankees, though not quite as much since Boston hadn't won a World Series in about 70 years. But now that I had inside access to the players and got to see a different side of them, I was becoming a closet Red Sox fan. Like the Royals, these guys were collectively a pleasant bunch to be around. Along with Dwight, one guy in particular I liked was Jim Rice.

Jim's career mirrored Dwight's in a lot of ways. He came up with the Red Sox organization in 1974 when he was 21. After playing a handful of games that year, he became a regular in 1975. He had four seasons with at least 39 home runs, and he would finish his career with a .298 batting average. He was finally elected to the Hall of Fame in 2009, a well-deserved and long-overdue honor.

Before the first game, Jim came down to the dugout and told Carmen and me to get our gloves. Mark Massey would later join us. Jim grabbed a bat and we went into foul territory near third base where we played pepper, a game in which a batter hits ground balls to a row of fielders at close range. Whoever fields the ball each time tosses it back like a pitch; the batter never touches the ball with anything but the bat. It's a way to loosen up the body and quicken the reflexes.

Jim played this with us before every game that series, and we cherished every second. Playing catch with players? Of course that was fun. Doing whatever tasks they asked us to do? We loved the responsibility of trying to come through for them. But to be able to say that Jim Rice, one of the game's most prominent sluggers, asked us to field ground balls from him every day for three straight days was larger than life to us.

Prior to the third game of the series, before we went down to the field, Jim asked Carmen and me and a couple of other clubhouse guys if we wanted to play the lottery with him. We would all throw in a few bucks and split whatever we won. This was the state lottery during a time when jackpots weren't nearly as rich as they are today, but this particular pot of $20 million was one of the largest in the game's brief history.

"Yeah, we'll do it!" we all said nearly in unison. We each contributed five dollars while Jim threw in $40 of his own, giving us 60 chances to win something. One of the clubhouse guys went out and bought the tickets.

That, for me, was the end of the story. I was so busy working after the game, I didn't see the tickets or check the numbers. I assumed we didn't win anything since nobody said anything.

Fast forward 30 years.

I ran into Carmen for the first time since we worked together. We stayed in touch on social media, but hadn't seen each other in person for more than three decades. We were reminiscing about our days with the Tribe and started talking about the Red Sox.

"Hey, you know what? Jim Rice still owes us money," Carmen said.

"What are you talking about?"

"Do you remember when we played the lottery with him?"

"Of course," I replied.

"Well, we won."

"No we didn't."

"Yeah, we did," he insisted. "I don't remember how many numbers we hit or how much it was, but we won, and Jim kept the money."

I love Carmen and I know he truly thinks we won, but I still don't believe him. First, I think that I would have heard chatter about it at the time from the other guys who chipped in. Second, Jim wasn't the kind of guy who would do something like that.

Or, I guess it's possible that Jim totally fooled me and it was all part of his pervasive scam: to travel to each city, gain the trust of batboys and ballboys by playing pepper with them, coax them out of a few bucks for the lottery to give himself extra chances to win, hit the jackpot, stop at the store on his way to the airport after the last game to redeem the winnings, and skip town with the loot.

But probably not.

Jim was a great player and person who gave us some fantastic memories. If we did win a few bucks and he kept it, I would prefer that he never pay me my share; the money would be spent quickly. But a story that begins with "Jim Rice still owes us money" is one that I can hang on to forever.

More Garbage Picking

Dave Stapleton played in the minor leagues for several seasons in the '70s before finally getting his chance with the Red Sox in 1980. He had a spectacular rookie season, batting .321 and coming in second for the AL Rookie of the Year award to Indians' slugger Joe Charboneau. He was Boston's starting first baseman in 1982 and 1983, and he was Bill Buckner's backup after that. The 1986 season would be Dave's final one in the majors.

Every Cleveland fan knew who Dave was because of his battle with Joe their rookie year. None of us liked Dave for no other reason than that, which in the sports world is perfectly acceptable. But we still respected how good he was, and even though he was no longer a starter with the Red Sox in 1986, he was still a noteworthy player to me.

Dave was about to head down to the field for batting practice before one of the games that series. He grabbed his batting glove from his locker, inspected it, and decided it was time for a new one. He turned away from his locker and took a couple of steps toward the garbage can to pitch it. I, coincidentally, happened to be standing in his path.

"Are you throwing that away?" I asked.

"Yeah, why?"

"Can I have it?"

He shot me an inquisitive look.

"Why?" he asked.

"I'd just like to have it," I replied.

He let out a sustained laugh while looking back and forth between me and the pine-tar-stained glove that absorbed days or even weeks of his hand sweat.

107

"I know," I said with a smile, acknowledging his unspoken bewilderment. "But you're a Major League player and I'm not, and that's your batting glove."

This was the Mike Mason incident all over again, except instead of a hat and a clubhouse attendant, it featured a batting glove and the player himself. Dave shrugged and finally handed it to me.

"Enjoy," he said.

"Thanks!" I replied, not quite showing the enthusiasm of the kid in the old Mean Joe Greene Coke commercial, but still excited, nonetheless.

Pretty lame story, right? Especially compared to some of the others you have read or will read. But it's a microcosm of everything that was glorious about my job. Yeah, it was just a batting glove from an average player, but every time I look at it all of these years later, it transports me to the best summer of my childhood. It reminds me of how fortunate I was to be part of something that so few kids get to experience. It also shows fans like you the humility that many players displayed behind closed doors. To Dave, the glove was trash. He couldn't understand how it could be anything more than that to anyone, until I expressed why I wanted it.

Uh-oh, can you feel another life lesson coming?

Don't ever underestimate the impact your stories or simple gestures (like giving a kid a dirty old batting glove) can have on others, no matter who you are or what position you hold. What may seem insignificant to you could have a powerfully positive effect on someone else, and you never know who that person may be or when or where it may occur. It's even possible that long after you've forgotten about it, maybe decades later, what you said or did may still resonate with that person. And to leave such a legacy to someone is pretty darn cool.

It's Just a Game

On February 27, 1986, there was a gas explosion at Milwaukee's new spring training facility in Chandler, Arizona. Ten people were injured, including manager George Bamberger and several of his coaches. All of them were hospitalized. They were burned on their hands, arms, faces, backs. Third base coach Tony Muser suffered burns over more than half of his body. That none of them died was nothing short of miraculous.

I was excited to see the Brewers, who came into town after the Red Sox. They made it to the World Series in 1982, losing to the St. Louis Cardinals in seven games. They had several well-known players in 1986, including Paul Molitor, Robin Yount, Cecil Cooper, Ben Oglive, Rob Deer, and Rick Cerone. But my heart sunk when I walked into the clubhouse before that first game. The first person I saw was one of the coaches. He had his shirt off. His back was to me, and it was covered in scars from the burns.

Until then, I forgot about the explosion. Unlike today, when every story is saturated by the media to the point that you know way more than anybody needs to know, I only read a couple of short newspaper articles when the blast initially occurred a few months earlier, and nothing since. Seeing that coach not only reminded me of what happened to them, it brought it to life. It shocked me, and I couldn't get the image out of my mind.

I would enjoy my time with the Brewers, but after that revelation in the clubhouse, I would look at them and all teams in a different light. Even though I realized before then that ballplayers and coaches were, in many respects, just like me, it was still difficult to not view them as being somewhat invincible because they were such strong, famous, talented men who played the nation's game at the highest level. The devastating injuries the Brewers suffered reminded me that baseball was simply what they did, not who they were.

The explosion reminded them of that, too.

"You see, sometimes in baseball we take every 2-2 pitch, every 3-2 pitch, every fly ball as life and death, but now I know it's not," Tony Muser told the L.A. Times in a July 23, 1986 article. "We don't always stop to think what a great life we have in baseball, whether we're the manager, star player, twenty-fourth man, or one of the coaches."

"You Dumb#$%!"

Cecil Cooper was not one of my favorite players because it seemed like he always killed the Indians, but because he came across through the media as a good guy and because he was so darn good, it was difficult not to respect him. Cecil broke into the league with the Red Sox in the '70s, but he was best known as the strong, left-handed, power-hitting first baseman for the Brewers for a decade. He was a five-time All-Star, two time league RBI champion, and 1983 recipient of the Roberto Clemente Award, which goes to a player who exemplifies kindness and sportsmanship.

Knowing his reputation for being a nice guy, I decided to ask a favor of him.

My cousin Frank and a few of his friends planned one evening to come to a Brewers' game, and they asked me if I could get them tickets. I knew Carmen and others in the clubhouse got tickets for their friends before, but I didn't know how. It turned out all they did was ask a player if they could use his allotted tickets for a game. Each visiting player received four tickets, but many went unused.

Before the game I looked at the list of ticket requests. It was on a sheet of paper on a clipboard in the middle of the clubhouse, and I noticed Cecil didn't sign up for any. I ran out to a payphone in the concourse and called Frank.

"Are you still coming to the game?"

"Yeah. Can you get us tickets?" he asked.

"I think I can. Let me call you right back."

I returned to the clubhouse and spent a few minutes trying to muster up the courage to ask Cecil if I could have his tickets. He was watching a couple of his teammates play cards when I nervously walked up to him.

"Mr. Cooper, if you're not using your tickets tonight, can I have them? I have some friends who would like to come."

Cecil was a soft-spoken man. Without taking his eyes off the card game, he mumbled, "Yes." *Dang, that was easy!* I thanked him, ran over to the sheet and marked down four tickets, and signed my name. I then dashed back to the concourse payphone to call Frank.

"I got you four tickets," I said. "They will be under your name. Tell the ticket person they were left by Cecil Cooper."

"What?" he exclaimed. "You got us Cecil Cooper's tickets?"

He didn't have to tell the ticket agent that they were from Cecil; I told him to mention it so that he could sound important.

I saw Frank at the game in his box seats behind home plate. He and his friends had a great time, and I was very grateful to Cecil for providing them with that opportunity. After the game, when I went up the tunnel with some of the equipment, Billy was waiting for me at the top of the steps outside the clubhouse door.

"What did you do?" he said in a loud and accusatory tone.

Uh-oh. I don't know, what did I do? My mind was racing. I couldn't think of anything. The Indians won. I caught every ball hit my way. I did all of my work before and during the game.

"Uh…what?" I said, as I set down the equipment.

"Who said you could have tickets?"

That's what this was about?

"Cecil Cooper did," I said confidently, throwing it right back at Billy.

"You dumb#$%!" he exclaimed. "If Cecil Cooper said you could have his tickets, then you should have signed Cecil Cooper's name on the request sheet, not yours!"

Gulp.

"Oh," I said sheepishly, feeling 100 percent like the name he'd called me.

"The team's traveling secretary saw it and asked me who Bill Croyle was," he said. "Players aren't supposed to give their tickets to someone else to give away. Cecil does something nice for you and you do something stupid like that?"

"Sorry," I said. I felt horrible, and Billy could sense it.

"Don't worry about it," he replied in an unusually calm voice. "I told him you were a dumb#$% and that you wouldn't do it again."

"Thank you," I said with a grin, never so happy to be called a dumb#$%. "Is Cecil in trouble?"

"Nah," he said. But, probably feeling like he was letting me off the hook a little too easily, his voice rose again. "Hey, where did you get the idea that you could ask players for their tickets anyway?"

"Carmen said…"

"Oh, Carmen said?" he interjected. "And you're going to listen to *that* dumb#$%?"

Great. Now I'd thrown Carmen under the bus.

"Listen to me, you are not allowed to ask players for tickets!"

"Okay, okay," I replied.

I turned and started down the steps to the tunnel to get more equipment.

"Hey!" Billy shouted.

My gosh, he's got to let this go! I stopped and swung my head back toward him. "What?" I exclaimed.

He was flashing me a rare smile and was calm again. "If you ever do ask another player for tickets again, make sure you sign their name, not yours."

I smiled and gave him a thumbs up.

Billy Sheridan passed away on August 5, 2007.

Sometimes we are fortunate to meet a person who makes a significant, lifelong impact on us in a short amount of time. I spent just six months of my life with Billy more than three decades ago, but I haven't forgotten him. Our outward personalities couldn't have been more different, but underneath that gruff exterior of his was a heart larger than life. The players loved him, the coaches loved him, and his employees loved him. He was a very good friend who made me mentally tougher, who reinforced in me the value of hard work, and who was responsible for many of my indelible memories from that dream season.

I wouldn't be shocked if, when I get to the gates of heaven, he casually greets me with a "Hey, dumb#$%." In fact, I'll be disappointed if he doesn't.

Bob Uecker

Bob Uecker is one of the funniest people on the planet. Known as the guy who did the hilarious Miller Lite commercials decades ago (you may recall his famous line, "I must be in the front rowwwww!"), who starred in the hit TV show *Mr. Belvedere* in the late '80s, and who had a significant role in the movie *Major League*, Bob has been announcing Brewers' games since 1971. If you have ever heard an interview with him or have had the opportunity to meet him, you know how much he loves to make people laugh.

Team announcers occasionally made appearances in the clubhouse before games. I had the pleasure of meeting a few, such as Hall of Fame pitcher and White Sox announcer Don Drysdale, Hall of Fame Tigers' announcer Ernie Harwell, and Bob. Bob never stopped with the one liners; anyone around him would walk away exhausted from laughing so hard. One moment in particular stands out.

I went up to the clubhouse to get some last-minute things for the dugout before the second game of the series. Bob was up there, as were some players who were about to head down to the field. The TV was tuned to the Indianapolis 500. The race was so popular back then that the Brewers had an Indy 500 pool. Each player threw some money into a pot and drew a random name of a driver. The winner got all the cash.

Bob was watching the pre-race coverage on TV when I stopped for a moment to watch with him. Suddenly, he yelled, "Oh no! Bobby Rahal crashed into the wall!"

Huh? We were watching the same thing. There was nothing to see. The race hadn't even started. But Bob knew what he was doing. One of the players, the one who had Rahal's name in the pool, came charging out of the training room.

"What the $%^&! He's out already?"

"Bahahaha!" Bob was so proud of himself. The player dropped his head down in shame and walked away. Who knows how many times he'd been had by Bob. I'm guessing every player in that clubhouse fell prey to his antics at least once.

I don't know how often today Bob is on the field before games, but if you're ever at a Brewers' game and get there early enough for autographs or photos, look for Bob and ask him to come over. I can't speak for him, but unless he has to be somewhere right away, I would bet that he'll acknowledge you. He will also have you in stitches, no matter how short your encounter is with him. Any interaction with any of the Brewers would be cool, but Bob Uecker is that organization's legend.

An Illusion

Before the third game of the series with the Brewers, their catcher Rick Cerone asked me if I wanted to play catch. Rick was a player that anyone who loved baseball knew, even though he wasn't a star. He broke into the league in 1975 with the Indians, then went to the Blue Jays, Yankees, Atlanta Braves, Brewers, back to the Yankees, Red Sox, back to the Yankees, across town to the New York Mets, and finally to the Montreal Expos (who later became the Washington Nationals). He played for 18 seasons, caught more than 100 games in only four of those seasons, had mediocre stats, but was good enough to make one heck of a career out of the game.

Our first few throws to each other during our catch were normal throws, but then he threw me a wicked knuckleball. I hadn't played catch with anyone who knew how to throw a real knuckleball consistently. I would have expected that if I had, it would have been with a pitcher, but it made sense that a catcher would know how to throw one, too. A good knuckleball does not rotate. It moves left to right and up and down, like a butterfly in the wind. Unlike any other pitch, such as a fastball or curveball, the catcher has no idea where it will ultimately go.

I put my glove out to catch Rick's throw, but the ball smacked me in the wrist below my glove and fell to the grass.

Rick busted out laughing.

"What's wrong, don't you know how to play catch?" he quipped.

I laughed as I threw it back to him, assuming his fun was over. But he was only beginning. The next throw came in a little harder. The ball moved in about six different directions. I ultimately positioned my glove to my right to backhand the ball…and it sailed right past me, completely untouched.

This was like playing catch with a magician, and the ball was nothing more than an illusion.

I chased it down and threw it back to Rick, wishing I practiced harder at throwing Charlie Hough's knuckleball so I could return the abuse. After he caught my regular lame throw, he came at me with the knuckler again. I extended my glove to my left. At the last second, the ball cut back and dropped, smacking me right in the gut.

"Awwww," I instinctively said as I doubled over.

Rick was having great fun. So were the guys playing catch next to us who laughed at the beating that I was taking. The fans who were watching must have been wondering how I was even allowed to be on a baseball field.

Rick threw me another one, a bit slower this time…and I finally caught it! Lucky? Well, if you try hard enough…

As much as I loved playing catch with players, I wanted out of that one. It was like being the last guy left in a dodgeball game against a dozen guys, each of them with a ball—a baseball—who smelled blood and showed no mercy. But I refused to quit. I didn't care how many bruises I would suffer. The story I wanted to be able to tell one day was that I played catch with Rick Cerone, not that I quit playing catch with Rick Cerone.

If you know someone who can throw a good knuckleball, ask them to throw it to you a few times. You will appreciate more what a catcher does behind home plate and what a batter has to face. Just make sure you wear a helmet. And some shin guards. And a chest protector. And facemask. And, if you're a guy, a cup. Definitely a cup.

Reggie! Reggie! Reggie!

Reggie Jackson.

There was no name, in my opinion, more synonymous with baseball in the '70s and into the early '80s. The right fielder played with five different teams starting in 1967, became known as Mr. October after those three homers in game six of the 1977 World Series against the Dodgers to clinch the title, and was still going strong in 1986 as a designated hitter for the California Angels (now the Los Angeles Angels).

Reggie was coming to Cleveland, and I was going to get to meet him. This was a baseball lover's dream come true.

The Indians took two of three from the Brewers, but then went to Boston for three and lost all of them. To be the best you have to beat the best, and the Indians weren't doing it. Their pitching wasn't horrible in that series, but they couldn't score runs. They lost 3-1, 5-1, and 6-4, dropped to 24-27 overall, and were 12 games out of first. But they returned the first week of June for a 12-game homestand. All of the games were against West Division teams: three each against the Angels, A's, Minnesota Twins, and Seattle Mariners. It was a chance for the Tribe to make a dent in the Red Sox lead.

The Angels had several other noteworthy players who were expected to help the team contend for the AL West Division title: Brian Downing, Doug DeCinces, Wally Joyner, Bob Boone, and Bobby Grich. But I truly did not care if I didn't meet, play catch with, talk to, get an autograph from, or even see any of those guys—as long as I got to meet Reggie and get his autograph.

There was, however, one daunting factor: Reggie's reputation of being a difficult person to deal with. He was outspoken. He was said to have a big ego. There were stories of him being rude to fans. He and Billy Martin, his manager when he was with the Yankees, frequently got into verbal spars and almost came to physical blows once in the dugout during a game in Boston in 1977. Eddie Murray and Kirk Gibson were both intimidating to me, but not until I was around them. Reggie was intimidating before he stepped foot in town.

To get his autograph, I figured I would have to play my cards perfectly by approaching him at the absolute right time. Maybe it would be after a game or two and he got acclimated to me being around him, or it might have to wait until after he had a good game. I probably couldn't get picky and ask him to sign it *to* me or on the sweet spot; I would have to take what I could get when I could get it.

But Carmen threw everything into chaos the very first day.

Reggie was sitting at his locker when I walked into the clubhouse, one of the few players there that early. He was intently reading a magazine, half dressed, his legs stretched out. It almost seemed like the perfect time to ask, but he looked too relaxed and engrossed in his magazine to bother him. So I changed into my uniform and went about my business, but I kept a ball and pen in my back pocket in case the opportunity presented itself.

About 20 minutes later, a reporter walked in and went to Reggie's locker. Watching them introduce themselves to each other and listening to the questions the reporter was asking, I could tell this was an interview for a national publication that was arranged in advance. That explained why Reggie was there so early ahead of the other players.

They were talking for a few minutes when Carmen arrived. I was standing by the television, about 10 feet from Reggie's locker.

"Oh, cool," Carmen said to me matter-of-factly. "Reggie's here."

"He's being interviewed," I said.

Carmen blankly looked at me, said nothing, and walked out the clubhouse. About 30 seconds later, he returned with a baseball and came back over to me.

"You got a pen?" he asked.

"For what?"

"I want Reggie's autograph."

"Are you kidding? You can't get it now!" I said incredulously, trying to keep my voice down so Reggie wouldn't hear me.

"Why not?"

"Because he's being interviewed."

"So?"

"I'm *not* giving you a pen. At least wait until he's done."

"C'mon!" he cried.

"No!"

So, Carmen went to look for one on his own. This terrified me to no end. All I wanted from that series was Reggie's autograph, and Carmen was about to make him angry and screw it up. You don't interrupt a temperamental player in the privacy of his clubhouse when he is in the midst of a one-on-one conversation with someone. I also did some homework: Reggie went hitless in their previous game at home against his former Yankees, a game in which the Angels only mustered one hit. This was absolutely *not* the time to ask him for an autograph. It broke every rule I had.

Fast forward about eight seconds.

Carmen found a pen.

Carmen was a big guy who used to play football, but I was still sizing him up as he walked toward Reggie, wondering if I could drag him down from behind. I was certain that for as much as I wanted Reggie's autograph, I could do it. Reggie might have even liked to have seen me do it. Seriously, I was mortified at what Carmen was about to attempt.

I stood back and watched as Carmen approached him. Reggie was in the middle of answering the interviewer's question when Carmen stepped right into it. There was no "Excuse me." No pause until Reggie was finished speaking. No "Mr. Jackson." Just...

"Hey Reggie, can you sign this for me?"

I cringed and looked away. This was awful. All of my research and knowledge about Reggie pointed to this becoming a very ugly scene. I waited for the screaming, the cursing, the threats...but all I heard was Reggie continue with his answer to the question from the reporter. I slowly turned my head and peeked...and there was Reggie holding Carmen's baseball, signing away.

He continued talking to the interviewer as he handed the signed ball back, not missing a beat. Carmen thanked him, turned and looked at me with a devious grin, and left the clubhouse.

What just happened?

Carmen broke every rule in my book for obtaining autographs, and with supposedly one of the most volatile guys in baseball, yet he walked away with the prize unscathed.

Now! I screamed in my head. *Get his autograph now!* I wasn't much of a rule breaker, even for my own made-up rules, but what was I waiting for? I pulled the ball and pen out of my pocket, thought about it for one more second, then followed Carmen's lead—I stopped thinking altogether. I walked up to Reggie and asked him if he would sign the ball (though I did wait for a slight pause in his interview *and* say "Excuse me" *and* call him "Mr. Jackson," as my rules dictated).

Without looking at me, continually keeping eye contact with the interviewer, Reggie took the ball and pen. I was in! So I decided to push a little further.

"Can you please sign it to Bill?"

He didn't answer. I didn't know if he heard me. Whatever. I would take what I could get.

And then the most beautiful thing happened.

Reggie turned the ball in a way so that he could sign "To Bill" over the laces right above the sweet spot…and then he signed his name across the sweet spot. I hadn't seen a player do that before. Normally, if I asked a player to sign it to me, he kept all of his writing confined to one area within the laces. Reggie signed it to me, *crossed over* the laces, and then signed his name on the sweet spot. Do I sound like a total baseball nerd? It was a breathtaking work of art.

The next day, before the second game of the series and pushing my luck, I asked Reggie to sign another ball, and he politely did. My grandfather was a volunteer with Shriners Hospitals for Children and they had an auction coming up to raise money. I surprised Grandpa with that ball for them to auction. It was the first and only time I would get an autograph to sell, but since all the money was going to Shriners, I didn't hesitate to do it.

And then came the third Reggie autograph. That's when I pushed him too far. A friend of mine asked me before the third game to get Reggie's autograph for him. I reluctantly agreed to try. After the game, which the Angels lost (they lost two of three that series), Reggie and the team were watching television as they waited for their bus to take them to the airport. This was my only chance to get his signature for my friend. I was breaking every rule: they lost, he was busy socializing with his teammates, and I already asked for a couple of autographs from him. I hesitantly approached him. As I thought might happen, he snapped.

"Are you serious, man?" Reggie said to me with an angry tone and disgusted look. "How many have I signed for you already?"

"I'm sorry," I said. "It's for a friend of mine who's a big fan of yours."

"This is ridiculous!" he replied. I wanted to run and hide.

"I'm sorry," I repeated. "Never mind."

Before I could walk away, Reggie snatched the ball and pen, scribbled his name, and shoved it back to me without further comment. I thanked him and moved as far away from him as I could. I didn't blame him for being upset. Every autograph I asked him for was for good reason. But three for one person, even though only one was for me, was a lot to ask from any player. My friend was ecstatic, though, when I gave it to him, so I was glad to have made the sacrifice.

The A's were coming to town next. It was time to get back to work *and* to follow my own rules for approaching players. Everything worked out with Reggie, but there was too much risk for my liking. I decided that next time, if necessary, I would go with my initial instinct and physically take down Carmen.

I Finally Get the Call

The Indians took three in a row from the A's, two of them on walk-off singles by Brett Butler and Mel Hall. It gave them a winning record again at 29-28 and moved them to within nine games of the Red Sox. Unfortunately, though, it was a crowded division. Baltimore, New York, and Milwaukee were also ahead of them, and Toronto and Detroit were only 1.5 and two games behind them, respectively.

I loved meeting the A's, especially veterans such as Dave Kingman, Dusty Baker, Carney Lansford, and Alfredo Griffin. But other than getting some autographs on a team ball, it was pretty much an uneventful series for me. The A's weren't very good that season and hadn't been good since the strike-shortened season in 1981. They would have three managers in 1986 and seemed to be trying to transition from older players to younger ones. It was a team going through some painful changes that would pay off with three straight World Series appearances from 1988 to 1990, including a World Series win in 1989. But, until then, they had to suffer a bit.

They had a young pitcher named Jose Rijo. He would eventually be traded to Cincinnati and win the World Series MVP in 1990 against, ironically, the A's. The team also had pitcher Dave Stewart, who came into the league with the Dodgers in 1978, but then went back to the minors for a couple of years. After playing for a few different teams, he would blossom in Oakland in 1987, his first of four consecutive 20-win seasons. Jose Canseco was the up-and-coming big name on the team. In 1986 he would hit 33 home runs, 117 RBI, and be named the AL Rookie of the Year.

The Ballboy

Some of my most favorite and fascinating stories of that season were when the A's would return to town in September with their future young stars. More on that to come.

The day after the A's left, the Indians hosted the Twins in the first of three games in front of the largest crowd of the season to date at 61,411 (thanks in large part to a Marathon Oil Co. promotion that gave a free ticket to anyone who bought at least eight gallons of gasoline). The Twins were worse than the A's. They would finish in sixth place that season, 21 games out of first place, though they had a few stars like Kirby Puckett, Kent Hrbek, and Bert Blyleven.

I got to the stadium a little late that day. When I walked into the laundry room, I noticed Carmen's bag wasn't there. I guess he would be late, too. I went into the clubhouse and all of the players were there and getting changed. Billy was sitting in a chair talking to one of them when he saw me.

"Hey, Bill," he shouted, one of the rare times he called me by my real name. He stood up and tossed me a Twins uniform. "Put this on."

"Why?"

"Carmen won't be here."

I was stunned. He hadn't missed a game all season.

"Where is he?"

"I don't know. Who the hell cares? You're up!"

Now I knew what it was like for a minor league player to be called up to the big leagues. *Don't ask questions, just go and do as you're told!* As I started toward the door to go to the laundry room to change, I was called by someone on the other side of the room.

"Hey, Bill…"

It was Kirby Puckett, the best player on the team and a future Hall of Famer. I hustled over to him. It was the first time we'd met; he obviously was paying attention when Billy called my name.

"Are you the batboy?" he asked.

"I am for tonight," I replied.

"That's cool," he said with his trademark smile. "I'm Kirby. I'll let you know if I need anything."

"Please do," I said.

126

I Finally Get the Call

I think Kirby thought I was a total rookie by my reaction to Billy throwing me the uniform, and he wanted to make me feel comfortable. Of course, nothing changed in my job except that I'd be in the dugout rather than on the field; I still had the usual pregame and postgame duties. But that's another example of how the stars were often the nicest guys toward me. That brief interaction with one of the game's greatest had enough of an impact on me that I still clearly recall everything about it today: what was said, when it was said, and even where we were standing. Fortunately, Billy called me by my real name. Hearing Kirby Puckett call me "Dumb#$%" the entire series would have been uncomfortable. Funny, but uncomfortable.

I found myself in quite a quandary during my first game as batboy. The crowd was electric, the Indians entered the game with a five-game winning streak, and they would thump the Twins that game, 11-2, to make it six wins in a row. I was cheering in my head with the crowd when Indians' designated hitter Andre Thornton belted a two-run single in the first, but on the outside I could show no reaction. When I was on the field wearing an Indians uniform, I could get excited. But I was now entrenched deep in enemy territory.

Meanball

Nearly all of the Twins' players and other personnel were low-key, nice guys who treated me well as batboy despite getting their butts kicked that night. But there were a couple of interesting and tense moments in the dugout that I wouldn't have witnessed or been part of had I been in my usual ballboy spot down the right field line. That's when I was enlightened to the major difference between the two jobs. My normal job had a buffer zone from most of the players; the batboy job didn't.

The first moment was about midway through the game when Indians' center fielder Brett Butler came up to bat. Brett was fast and known for dropping bunts down the third base line since he could often beat out the third baseman's throw to first. I was sitting on the bench during this particular at-bat next to one of the Twins' coaches. This coach hadn't said a word the entire game. Having trailed by a lot since early in the game, there wasn't much to be said. But when Brett came up, the coach let loose.

"Hey, Butler, why don't you go ahead and bunt since you can't hit!" he screamed. The Twins were down eight runs at the time, so there was certainly a lot of frustration. But this was my first experience hearing a coach yell at an opposing player. Maybe the two had a history with each other; I don't know. But this coach was burning mad. Brett ignored him the entire at-bat, though there is no doubt he heard him.

"Do you even know how to swing the bat?" the coach cried. "Do you want me to come out and show you?"

I wondered if the manager, other coaches, or any players would tell him to stop, but they all stood stoned-faced and intently watched the game as he continued to yell. That's something I noticed about coaches and players: if

129

one of them was upset, everyone else usually stayed out of his way and let him throw his tantrum. The coach was relentless toward Brett throughout the at-bat.

"You're awful! You can't get a real hit! Go ahead and bunt!"

And on that note, Butler dropped a beautiful bunt right down the third base line for a hit. I watched Brett when he got to first base to see if he would make a gesture toward or even look at the coach, but he didn't. The coach said his peace, Brett absorbed it, and the coach left Brett alone the rest of the game. Just as quickly as it started, it was over.

The second incident directly involved me and was instigated by Billy Beane. Billy was a guy I hadn't heard of until the Twins came to town. I saw him at his locker in the clubhouse, but he seemed to keep to himself the whole series. What I didn't know about him was his interesting background.

Billy was a first round pick of the Mets in 1980 and was projected to be a star. He gave up a scholarship from Stanford in order to join the club. He played in the minors the first six years with the exception of about a dozen games at the big league level. He came to the Twins in 1986 where he split time between the minors and majors. In about 80 games with the Twins that season he would hit .213. Up until this night, his big league average for the season was around .170.

He didn't start the game, but he substituted late for left fielder Mickey Hatcher. Unaware that the substitution was made, I got out Hatcher's bat when he was due up first in the top of the ninth, but I happened to glance at the lineup card taped to the wall of the dugout and realized Billy was in. I quickly put Hatcher's bat away and grabbed Billy's. When I turned around, Billy already had his helmet on and was waiting for his bat.

"Why didn't you have my bat ready?" he snapped. He wasn't kidding. He was angry.

"Sorry," I said. "I didn't realize you were in." I cringed as those words exited my mouth and entered his ears. That was the worst thing I could have said to him, especially since he'd been struggling at the plate.

"Next time have my bat ready for me when it's my turn to bat!"

"I will," I said out loud.

You're a jerk, I said in my mind.

Billy went up to face Tom Candiotti. Tom was three outs away from a complete game, and he struck out Billy swinging on a nasty knuckleball that Billy probably wouldn't have hit if he'd been given 10 chances at it. Nobody was happier than I to see him whiff. When Billy returned to the dugout, I put my hand out for the bat. When players struck out, a lot of times they put away their own bats. To my surprise, Billy politely handed his bat to me along with his helmet. He looked about as low as I'd ever seen a player look. He didn't say a word. He found a seat on the bench and dropped his head into his hands.

Okay, now I felt for him. And in hindsight, knowing his full story and all of the expectations that hadn't come to fruition, I can understand his frustration. It likely wasn't one night of frustration or even a season's worth; it was probably several seasons of not reaching the goals he'd set out to attain or the expectations that people had for him. I doubt that he was upset that I didn't have his bat ready. Had he been hitting .300 and in his fifth full season in the big leagues, as he probably expected several years earlier would be the case, I don't think he would have yelled at me.

Billy would end his playing career a few years later and become a scout for the A's. He would work his way up to general manager in 1997, and he is the executive vice president today. The book and movie *Moneyball* are based on Billy's use of statistical analysis to build the low-payroll A's into perennial contenders.

While Billy hasn't won a World Series running the A's, I would like to see him do it one day. I think he deserves it with all of the effort he's put in and the risks he's taken in his unique and successful approach to building a team, which other teams have copied with success. So long as he doesn't have to go through the Indians in the playoffs, of course.

I Made a Kid Happy

A lot of people thought I looked like Brett Butler. Not just my mom or a couple of friends. At least once a week through the entire season I was summoned by fans during batting practice to come over to the railing to sign their programs or baseballs, or to take a picture with them, because they thought I was Brett. He was about three inches taller and had about 40 pounds on me, but he was still a small guy compared to other players. In our uniforms and from a distance, maybe there were similarities. I wasn't even convinced of that until one game my cousins attended. I found out afterward that one cousin told the other that she didn't know I was left handed. I'm not. The guy she thought was me playing catch with another player during batting practice was Brett.

After an Indians' win earlier in the season, Brett was asked to do a radio interview with the visiting team's announcers. He sat in the visitors' dugout with headphones on waiting for them to come back from a commercial when he saw me cleaning up.

"Hey, what size shoe do you wear?" he asked.

Ha! It was him! The foot fetish employee who called me at the start of the season! Okay, probably not, but how weird that I was asked that question for the second time that season.

"Eight and a half."

"I think I could fit into those," Brett said.

I laughed. "You'd be shocked at how many people think I am you. I'm asked to sign your autograph all the time."

"I hope you're signing it," he said, looking like he meant it.

"Oh, no, I wouldn't do that."

"Why not? Go ahead! Sign!"

133

"I wouldn't feel right," I said.

"Hey, if it makes a kid happy, that's all that matters."

If you received an autograph from Brett Butler at a game in 1986 and are worrying that I may have been the one to sign it…don't. I never signed his name. Anytime anyone asked me to sign something, I first made it very clear who I was. That prompted some to say, "Oh, never mind." But 12 of them didn't. Yes, I signed 12 autographs that season, and I was fine with 11 of them. But there was one that I absolutely didn't want to sign, so much so that I almost resorted to finally signing Brett's name.

It was right before the second game of that series with the Twins. Carmen was back, so I returned to being the ballboy. I came out of the dugout to take my position in right field when a little kid, about seven or eight years old, called me from the stands to the left of the dugout.

"Hey, Indians guy, will you sign this ball for me?" he yelled.

"I have to get out to right field," I said, as the umpires and managers had their customary meeting at home plate to exchange lineup cards.

"Pleeeeease," he pleaded. His older sister, probably about my age, was with him. I went over to them to explain that I wasn't a player.

"I don't care!" the boy said sternly as he shoved the ball and pen toward me.

I reluctantly took them. It looked like a clean ball, but as I rotated it, I noticed it had one signature on it: Bert Blyleven.

Bert broke into the big leagues in 1970 and pitched for four seasons in the '80s with the Indians. He had one of the nastiest curveballs I had ever seen and was, in my opinion, one of the best pitchers in the game. He would finish his 22-year career with 287 wins and a 3.31 ERA. He was, I felt, a future Hall of Famer.

When I saw his name on the boy's ball, I froze. With the game about to start, my signature would likely be the last one this boy would get. With only Bert Blyleven on there, no way was I going to add my name to it.

"Oh…I can't sign this," I said. "You have Bert Blyleven's autograph on here. He's a great player."

"I don't care," the boy repeated.

The managers were heading back to their dugouts and the players were taking the field. The game was about to start. I had to decide what to do. I looked at his sister, hoping she'd back me up on this.

"Please don't make me sign this," I said.

"C'mon!" the boy said, clearly irritated.

"Will you *just* sign the ball?" his sister implored. She was losing patience with both of us. "This is what my brother wants."

I thought for a moment about signing Brett's name. What would be worse: a ball with a real Bert Blyleven and a fake Brett Butler, or a ball with a real Bert Blyleven and a real Bill Croyle? Take a moment to debate that in your own mind if you'd like. I couldn't decide. Neither option was good, in my opinion, so I sort of compromised. I turned the ball to the opposite side of where Bert's name was and signed my own name in the smallest handwriting I possibly could. I gave it to the boy, and he was ecstatic.

"Thank you! Thank you!" he exclaimed. His sister smiled at me and repeated his sentiments.

In 2011, Bert Blyleven was elected to the Hall of Fame. That means somewhere today there is a guy in his 40s with an autographed Bert Blyleven baseball wondering, *Who the $%^& is Bill Croyle?* But I have accepted that that's okay, because Brett was right. At the time, I made a kid happy, and that's all that matters.

Tobacco Gum

The Indians' winning streak ended at six. They lost the second and third games to Minnesota and the first one to Seattle before winning the last two. At the end of the 12-game homestand, the Indians were 32-31, 10.5 games out of first place. So they gained 1.5 games on the Red Sox over that stretch. It was better than losing ground, but not as much as they hoped to make up. It felt like they were treading water. Pat Tabler was out with an injury. Tony Bernazard and Joe Carter were hitting over .300, but Andre Thornton was struggling at .224 and Cory Snyder was *really* struggling at .174. The pitching would be stellar one day and lay an egg the next. They needed to figure out a way to get over that hump and win with more consistency.

Seattle, like Oakland, wasn't a team swirling with a lot of excitement, from my perspective. They would finish in last place that season. They did have some decent players, such as Danny Tartabull, Harold Reynolds, Jim Presley, and Steve Yeager, whose cousin Chuck Yeager was the first pilot to break the speed of sound in flight in 1947. I read *The Right Stuff* my freshman year, so I was intrigued to meet one of Chuck's close relatives. But this was not a team with any prospective Hall of Fame players or postseason potential.

I hung out a bit before each of the games with Mariners' relief pitcher Pete Ladd. He was instrumental in the Brewers' success when he played for them in 1982 and they made it to the World Series. But his personality, not baseball stature, is why I enjoyed being around him. He kept things loose in a losing clubhouse and didn't take himself or anyone else too seriously.

One thing I recall about him, because it's difficult not to forget something this odd, is that he took big wads of chewing gum and tobacco and stuffed both into his mouth at the same time. It was as appalling as it sounds.

I saw him do it in the clubhouse and assumed it was a one-time thing he did just to gross out a teammate, but he did it again before another game when we were in the dugout.

"Why?" I asked as he inserted sizeable chunks of each into his mouth.

He chewed them together, opened his mouth, and pulled out a huge pink and black wad, admiring his creation.

"I chew both, so why not both at once?" he replied proudly.

After Pete was released from the Mariners in 1987 and couldn't get any offers from any teams, he took out an ad for $260 in the USA Today with the phrase "Have fastball, will travel," hoping to land a job with another club. Like his tobacco gum, he always had crazy ideas that he wasn't afraid to try. He told Washington Post writer Tony Kornheiser at the time about his ad: "It might turn out to be the greatest investment I ever made, and if not, it was fun." He never did latch on with another team, but it certainly wasn't for lack of trying. A lot of players and people in general could learn a lot from Pete. Not about the tobacco gum, but about attitude. He may have lost his job, but he kept it in perspective and didn't lose his sense of humor.

One other story from the Mariners' visit that was intriguing to me as a baseball lover occurred after the second game with Seattle. Harold Reynolds, their leadoff hitter and generally a very reliable one, was in a slump. He was three for 24 in his last five games and his average was down to .229. After the game, Carmen and I packed up the bats and headed to the tunnel. About a quarter of the way up the tunnel was Harold. He was sitting across the walkway, his back against the wall on the right side with his legs extended across to the left side, right in our path. He was mumbling to himself, visibly frustrated. He had his hands positioned as if he were holding a bat, trying to figure out his grip and swing.

I made three trips between the dugout and clubhouse, having to step over him each time. I'm not even sure he noticed me. He sat there for a long while, missing the team bus and having to take a cab back to the hotel. I was enthralled to see this game psychologically affect someone so much. Not that I didn't know it could—I don't know of any sport that messes with your mind more than baseball. But to see a player separate himself from his teammates and coaches to try to talk himself through his struggles was captivating. It was also more proof that no matter how much money you make, if you don't perform at the level you know you are capable of, it is going to take a mental toll on you.

I can't imagine Harold got much sleep that night, but his time alone in the tunnel paid off, at least in the short term. He went two for four the next day and left the tunnel clear for us to walk.

That Chicken Is a Bit Overdone

The Tribe went on a 12-game road trip to face the same four teams they'd just played on their homestand, and they went 8-4. It was much better than most fans expected. The offense was fairly consistent. The pitching, as usual, was all over the board, from giving up a single run one game to eight or nine the next. When they returned home for a three-game series against the Royals starting July 4, they were 40-35, 9.5 games behind first-place Boston, and in third place (New York was in second, eight games out). Amazingly, the Indians still had an outside shot at the division title.

Every team would visit Cleveland twice that season, and the Royals were the first to return for their second stint. Unfortunately, George Brett was injured and didn't make the trip. It was nice to see the other guys again, but not having George there was a huge disappointment. On the bright side, the Indians would take all three games and move to within eight games of first.

With home runs from Cory Snyder and Andre Thornton, the Tribe won that Friday night game, 10-3, in front of 73,303 fans, the largest crowd since 1973. It also put the season attendance at 683,323 through just 38 games, surpassing the total 1985 season attendance. The evening featured the defending champions, fireworks, Phil Niekro on the mound, and the world-famous San Diego Chicken.

For those who don't know the Chicken, it is a mascot played by a man named Ted Giannoulas that started in the early 1970s at San Diego events. The Chicken became a national phenomenon in the 1980s and has made more than 5,000 appearances nationally and internationally. His popularity was the catalyst for many professional team mascots across the country. In fact, he was named by *The Sporting News* as one of the Top 100 Most Powerful People in

Sports in the 20th Century. It sounds crazy, but he really was *that* big of a deal, and I would bet the biggest reason—even bigger than the Indians and Royals—for the large crowd that night.

The Chicken entertained Indians fans with his usual tricks, stunts, and pranks throughout the game. Afterward, when we were finished with our work in the clubhouse, Carmen and I headed to the Indians' clubhouse where we were going to spend the night (more on that in a minute). It was there where I met Ted out of his chicken costume, which was being washed. Ted was telling us stories about his job when Cy emerged from the laundry area looking as white as a baseball. He was holding something in his hands, but I couldn't make out what it was.

"Hey, Ted," he said, "Was this not supposed to go in the dryer?"

There was a collective gasp from everyone in the room when we figured out what Cy was holding: a big pile of feathers. It was—or had been—Ted's costume. The Chicken was dead.

"Ummm…no…it wasn't supposed to go in there," Ted said calmly. We waited in silence for Ted's next reaction to his alter ego being destroyed.

He busted out laughing.

Fortunately, Ted had an extra costume with him. The Chicken was still kickin', and the color in Cy's face returned.

More than 30 years after that incident, I emailed Ted to ask him if he remembered it. Given the thousands of events he's done over the decades, I didn't expect him to. But, shockingly, he recalled it even more vividly than I had.

"Yes, I remember the situation and you're correct, I wasn't upset but rather disappointed in myself for forgetting to tell the clubhouse attendant, Cy Buynak, or his assistant, not to use the dryer for the outfit. The furry fabric was far too delicate for heat and would shrink. The body suit was totally ruined as a result. Luckily, I always carried a backup costume and had one ready to go for my game the following evening.

"Normally, I would wash the outfit personally at the hotel or a local laundry mat," he continued. "But since Cy insisted he could take care of it—players' uniforms notwithstanding—I relented. He was always friendly and cordial, never accepting a nickel from me for his services during any of my visits. He felt badly when he saw my expression after the wash, I'm certain. But I assured Cy that it was my fault since the stadium didn't have a birdbath around!"

If you've ever wondered what happened to the Chicken, his biography and FAQs on his website, famouschicken.com, are worth the read. He has performed in all 50 states, is still the only Chicken (he never franchised it), and he still does about 75 events a year (he did 250 to 275 annually in his younger days).

After the Chicken and everyone else left for the night, Carmen, Mark, and I stayed; we were spending the night in the Indians' clubhouse. It wasn't unusual for some of the clubhouse guys, especially Billy and Cy, to stay over after a long night game and with an afternoon game the next day. Wanting to be able to say we spent a night in the stadium, the three of us received permission to do so from Cy "as long as you guys behave! And if you don't…!" Yeah, yeah, we knew the drill.

It was after midnight by the time everyone left. We borrowed a pair of Joe Carter's socks from his locker, rolled them into a ball, grabbed some players' bats and helmets (because you need to wear a helmet when you're using a sock ball), and played clubhouse baseball. We were in the midst of our game at about 1 A.M. when we heard noise around the corner near the clubhouse door.

"What was that?" I asked.

"Probably a stadium worker cleaning up," Carmen said. There was a large contingency that worked throughout the night cleaning the stadium of all the trash, which was a considerable amount after a crowd like the one we had that night.

When we got tired of playing inside, we decided to go down to the field to hit and field some balls. Yeah, it was dark, but if you had the chance to play on a Major League field, would it really matter whether or not you could see? I grabbed a couple of bats and balls and went over to the clubhouse door.

One problem: the door wouldn't open.

"Hey, how do I open this?" I yelled across the clubhouse.

Carmen came over.

"It's locked," he said nonchalantly.

"What do you mean 'locked?' Who locked it? How do we get out?"

Then it hit Carmen. That noise we'd heard earlier…it was a stadium worker *locking the clubhouse door!* Yes, it locked from the outside, and we couldn't unlock it from the inside. How did they not know we were in there?

Carmen and I banged on the door, screaming for someone to let us out, but our cries fell on deaf ears. With the entrance to the tunnel on the other side of the door, we were locked in for the night. I assume that wouldn't meet fire code standards today. I wonder if it even did back then.

We played more clubhouse baseball and talked about life before I finally laid down on the training table at 4 A.M., though I didn't fall asleep until about 5:30 A.M. given that a training table is one of the most uncomfortable things to sleep on. I was woken about 90 minutes later by the sound of the clubhouse door unlocking. It was one of the stadium workers.

"Hey, what are you doing in here?" the startled woman yelled.

"We're the batboys and ballboys. We spent the night here," I mumbled as I sat up.

"Who said you could do that?"

"Cy did. Except we didn't know we'd be locked in."

"Who locked you in?"

"I don't know. Someone locked the door last night without checking to see if anyone was in here."

She paused for a moment.

"Bahahaha! You got locked in? That's funny!"

"Yeah, funny," I said, trying unsuccessfully to smile.

"Well, you're free now! Have fun!"

I was so tired, but I decided to take her advice. With Carmen and Mark still asleep, I went down the tunnel and out to the field by myself. It was about 7 A.M. —and it was magnificent.

The field and stands were deserted. It was the first time I'd experienced such tranquility in the stadium. The sun was starting to rise over the scoreboard. The temperature was probably in the mid-60s. A light breeze was blowing in from the lake. Seagulls squawked as they soared above. I wasn't a runner, but I jogged a lap around the track just to do it. When I returned to the dugout, I sat on top of the steps for about 30 minutes and soaked in the beauty of the moment, thinking about all of the baseball greats who once sat where I was sitting.

A few weeks earlier my friend Ron and I saw a new movie called *Ferris Bueller's Day Off*, still one of my all-time favorites. In the movie, Ferris said, "Life moves pretty fast. If you don't stop and look around once in a while, you could miss it." It was incredible to me how I worked in that stadium for dozens of games that season and was in it dozens of times as a fan before that, and yet on this morning I saw it in a light I hadn't seen before and would never see again. The serenity was breathtaking.

I went back inside the clubhouse to try to sleep, but after that time on the field, my mind was awake and ready to start the day.

The game on Saturday was in the afternoon, and it was the first time all season that I didn't want to be there. The temperature hit close to 90 degrees, it was humid, and there was very little breeze. There was a family of four sitting behind me that complained about the heat the entire game; they brought no sunblock and were burnt to a crisp. It was so hot and I was so tired that I closed my eyes between innings and a couple of times almost didn't wake up. After the game I got home and forgot that I told Ron I'd go to the theatre with him to see the new action movie *Top Gun*. I made it through most of the movie, but I dozed toward the end. I'm probably the only person ever to fall asleep in the theatre during *Top Gun*.

But I'm also one of the few people to ever wake up on a summer morning in Cleveland Stadium and take a jog around the field at sunrise. For that alone, it was worth it.

And I still haven't seen the ending to *Top Gun*.

I Didn't See Any Drugs

Family, friends, neighbors, friends of friends, and a multitude of others thought I had the coolest job in the world...except one person.

My mom was a teller at a local bank when a guy she knew walked in.

"So, I hear your son is working for the Indians," he said.

"Yes," my mom said. "He's loving it."

"Well, I imagine it has you pretty concerned."

"Concerned? About what?"

"The drugs," he said.

"The drugs?"

"Oh yeah, all those guys do drugs," he said, as if he were an authority on the subject. "I'd be real worried about letting my kids around any pro athletes."

"Well," my mom said, trying to stay diplomatic, "I'm pretty sure that they all don't do drugs, and those who do probably don't do them in front of him."

"I don't know," the guy replied, unconvinced.

Among the more than 400 players and coaches I would come in contact with that season, I did not see a single one do drugs, I was not approached by one to do drugs, none of them acted like they were on drugs, nor did I see any drugs or drug paraphernalia in their lockers. And only once was I suspicious.

It was before an evening game. I will leave out the team name because it was pure speculation on my part. The public address announcer was introducing the person singing the National Anthem, which meant the game was just a couple of minutes away from starting. Carmen and I were getting ready to walk to the top of the steps with the rest of the players for the anthem when one of the players commented that they needed more cups for the Gatorade. It was a hot day and the players went through a lot of cups during their pregame warmups. After the anthem I sprinted up the tunnel, into the clubhouse, and back into the training room. Except for a couple of workers who were cleaning, the clubhouse was empty and quiet. I grabbed the cups and was heading out when I saw something quite peculiar: all four bathroom stall doors were closed and occupied by players. Not a sound was coming from any of them. I could see all eight cleats. They were as still as could be.

Never had I noticed a player, let alone four, not in the dugout or bullpen during the National Anthem. And not that I was the bathroom monitor, but I never saw all four stalls occupied at one time. The first pitch was going to be thrown in a minute or two and yet four guys were as motionless as mannequins, completely silent, going to the bathroom? Possibly, but not likely. Whatever was going on in there, be it something illegal or four simultaneous cases of constipation, it was none of my business and surely something they neither needed nor wanted an audience for. I brought the cups down and took my position on the field.

We have all met people like the guy who came into my mom's bank. No matter how happy you may be about something, there will always be a cynic to try to bring you down, maybe because of jealousy or a lack of education. Of course some athletes did drugs. So did countless people in other professions. To think that athletes did them on a larger scale or more frequently or in the open was absurd. And if I encountered anything like that, my parents trusted that they raised me well enough to know right from wrong.

Shannon

After the series against the Royals, the Indians went to Chicago and lost two of three, then they came home and split four games with Texas. It was during that Texas series that I met Shannon.

Fans approached me during nearly every game. Most wanted baseballs. Some wanted me to get them autographs from players. Others wanted my autograph. One was a Mormon who gave me a pamphlet and spent nine innings trying to recruit me to her church. Some were just outgoing people who struck up normal conversations with me.

And then there was Shannon.

About my age, Shannon was sitting with her girlfriend in box seats in the section behind me, several rows back. They both came down at the end of the first inning to say hi. Shannon was attractive with short brown curly hair and a pretty smile. Both girls visited me every inning or two, though Shannon took much more of an interest in me. I wasn't too seasoned in asking out girls, but this seemed like a no-brainer given how much she was paying attention to me. Needing a few innings to find the courage, I figured I'd ask her at the end of the game when there weren't any other fans around.

Late in the game, around the seventh or eighth inning, a foul ball was hit my way, my first of the game. I scooped it up and sat down. Shannon's friend came running down from her seat by herself.

"Hey, Bill, can I have that ball?"

Indians' executives sat in the press boxes above home plate each game. There was one guy in particular who sat on the far left side who I was told was in charge of us and watched our every move. I'd never met him and didn't know what he looked like, but my source was solid, so I paid attention to when

149

he was there and when he wasn't. On this particular night he wasn't, so I gave her the ball.

"Thank you!" she exclaimed as she excitedly ran back to her seat.

But that warm feeling I'd always gotten when I was able to make a fan happy evaporated in seconds.

"What did you do that for?" came a shout from right behind my ear. It was Shannon.

"Do what?" I asked, stunned to see her looking so upset.

"Why did you give her that ball?"

"Because she asked for it."

"What about me?" She was angry. Like I said, I didn't have much experience asking girls on dates. In hindsight, it would have been smart of me to hang on to that ball and give it to Shannon when I planned to ask her out. Duh, right? But if a ball meant that much to her, wouldn't she have run down with her friend to ask me for it?

"If another one is hit to me I'll give it to you," I said.

"What if there isn't another one?"

"I can still get you a ball from the dugout," I said.

"But I wanted *that* one!"

"I'm sorry. She asked, so I gave it to her. Isn't she your friend?"

"Yeah, but *I* wanted a ball! Why do you think I've been talking to you all night?"

Ding! Ding! Ding!

And there it was. At least the Mormon girl had a deep-rooted spiritual reason for talking to me the entire game and didn't hide that fact. Shannon just wanted a baseball. I felt as used and bruised as the baseball that I'd given to her friend.

"So you've been talking to me all night just to get a ball?"

She stomped away without answering.

"Boy, she's a nice girl, huh?" a lady sitting in the row behind me who witnessed the exchange said facetiously. "Don't worry about her, she's not worth your time."

Shannon

I'd be lying if I said Shannon's reaction toward me didn't sting, but I got over it the next inning when a second ball was hit my way. I caught it and sat down. Within a few seconds, as I expected, Shannon was behind me with a big smile.

"Can I have that one?" she asked.

"I'm sorry," I said. "I forgot that I'm only allowed to give away one each game."

Zing!

If Shannon's eyes were lasers, I would have been vaporized on the spot. She mumbled something I can't print and left in a huff. When she was out of sight and gone forever, I turned to the nice lady sitting behind me who had expressed remorse for me earlier after the way Shannon treated me.

"Here you go," I said, as I handed her the baseball. "And thank you."

French Fries and a Foul Mouth

The Indians were nine games out of first place after that series with Texas. Their next 11 games—four at Kansas City, three at home against Chicago, and four in Texas—would produce a 6-5 record. But, thanks to Boston winning just a couple of games on a long west coast trip during that period, the Indians would climb to fourth place and cut Boston's lead to 5.5 games. The Yankees, Orioles, Indians, Tigers and Blue Jays were all within 4.5 games of each other. The Indians' next eight games at home against Detroit and New York were expected to be some of the biggest in the team's recent history. It was the last week of July and the Indians were still in the race for the division crown, something that hadn't happened during my lifetime.

But the excitement vanished quickly.

We lost the first game to the Tigers, 5-1, as Jack Morris and reliever Bill Campbell shut them down.

The second game? A 6-3 defeat in 11 innings as the bullpen couldn't finish a solid start by Phil Niekro.

Game three was really ugly. Detroit erupted for eight runs in the fifth, sixth, and seventh innings for an 11-3 win.

In the fourth game, the Indians were down 7-4 going into the bottom of the eighth when they scored four times off Bill Campbell, all on singles and doubles, to pull out a shocking 8-7 win. It was an exciting comeback and a much-needed victory, but it was disappointing that it was the only game they could salvage. They didn't lose much ground, as they were now six games behind Boston, but they let a great opportunity to close the gap slip away.

In the first game, Kirk Gibson hit a home run and got on base three times. The win was big for them, as it moved them to within a game of the Indians.

After the game the team celebrated. The clubhouse was louder than ever. The players ate ribs and French fries for dinner, laughed a lot, and talked with the media. One television station, I assume from Detroit, was there. As the reporter was wrapping up his interview with a player near Kirk's locker, Kirk yelled at the top of his lungs to our clubhouse manager, "Hey, Billy, where are the $%^&*@# French fries?" He was just giving Billy a hard time, but he dropped the obscenity while they were still doing the interview.

"Oh, sorry," Kirk said with a sheepish grin when the interviewer told him what he'd done.

I couldn't stop laughing. When Kirk turned his head toward my direction and saw my reaction to his faux pas, his grin turned into a huge smile as if to say, "Yeah, kid, that *was* pretty funny, wasn't it?"

And there was the moment I'd been waiting for, the one that hadn't materialized when they were in town opening day weekend. Kirk and I finally connected. It was in the most unexpected way—over fries and a curse word—but so what! I'd just been welcomed into his world.

I dashed out to my bag and grabbed a ball and pen. After Kirk was finished eating his ribs and $%^&*@# French fries, I got my autograph.

Covering Second Base

Before the second game of the series, with a couple of players electing to handle cutoff duties during batting practice and with the outfield crowded, I decided to take a shot at fielding grounders at second base. Several weeks earlier, Mark Massey and I fielded some balls at third base. Mark was a natural infielder, so he handled them pretty well. I was a solid outfielder who liked to play infield, but I wasn't as good as Mark. I learned that day why third is called the "hot corner" as balls shot at me like missiles. A coach finally told us both to get out of there before we got killed.

Playing second base, on the other hand, was much safer given that it's several more feet from home plate and most balls are slowed by the infield grass. I was doing well, scooping up every one that came my way and even making a few nice backhands when, suddenly, two balls came at me in rapid succession. But only one came off the batter's bat.

Where did that other ball come from?

I fielded both of them and tossed them behind the pitcher. Immediately after the batter took a swing at the next pitch and hit the ball to left field, another ball came toward me. Again, I fielded it and looked around. Was someone messing with me? As I was getting ready to throw it back to the pitcher, I saw a hand to the left of the batting cage waving.

Me? I gestured. He nodded, so I threw the ball in to him. After the batter swung at the next pitch and hit it to the outfield again, that guy hit another grounder to me.

Oh crap! I finally realized who it was and what was happening. It was Lou Whitaker, the Tigers' All-Star second baseman. Because I was at his position, he decided to hit some balls to me.

155

For the next 10 minutes or so I was like Lou's protégé at second. I would occasionally have to field a ball from the batter in the cage, but after each swing, assuming the ball didn't come my way, Lou would hit one to me.

"Thanks for the ground balls!" I said to him afterward in the dugout.

"Oh, no problem," he said in his soft, unassuming voice.

This may not rank a whole lot higher than the Dave Stapleton story in terms of excitement, but it ranked as one of the best moments of the season for me. While I was nervous about looking like a fool in front of one of the greatest ever to play the position, I had so much adrenaline flowing that nothing was going to get past me. This was like a lover of science getting to work with Stephen Hawking, or someone who loves to cook getting to make a meal with Chef Michael Symon, or you getting to do whatever it is that you love to do with one of the best in that profession.

Lou was the AL Rookie of the Year in 1978. He was a five-time All-Star, collected more than 2,300 hits, and won three Gold Gloves. He and Alan Trammell, the Tigers' shortstop, played together from 1978 to 1995, forming one of the best and longest double-play combos in history. Lou could hit for average, hit for power, steal bases...he was the consummate leadoff hitter and a force behind the Tigers' World Series championship season in 1984.

Lou is not in the Hall of Fame, even though his statistics are in line with many other second basemen who are in. Baseball historian Bill James named him the thirteenth best second baseman of all time. Personally, all biases aside, he should be in based on his statistics. And if you factor in his personality and heart, it's a slam dunk.

Ernie Harwell

During that series with the Tigers, before one of the games, I was in the clubhouse when I heard a voice from the other side of the room. I knew immediately that it was Ernie Harwell.

Growing up in the '70s and '80s, radio was big. Big for music, big for news, and big for sports. I had an AM-only clock radio on the floor next to my bed. Each night I would listen to the Indians or Cavs on 1100 (WWWE then, WTAM today) as I fell asleep. If they weren't playing, I would scan the dial to see what other games I could find. Without cable television and games to watch around the clock like we can today, finding a game live on the radio in another city was exciting, like entering a different dimension. It's something kids today cannot even fathom.

The easiest games to get outside of Cleveland were Tigers' games because Detroit was only about 175 miles away. Since the dial on my radio was just that—a dial and not digital, it was often difficult to see if I had the right station, so I would listen for Ernie's voice.

Ernie broadcasted baseball since the 1940s and for the Tigers since 1960. He had a very distinctive sound that left no question to the listener that it was him. I was anxious to meet him, so when I heard him across the clubhouse, I didn't waste any time approaching him with a baseball.

"Hi, Mr. Harwell. May I please have your autograph?"

He looked at me, silent for a moment.

"What? You want *my* autograph?"

"Yes, sir."

"Wow. What is your name, son?"

He still hadn't taken the ball.

"I'm Bill. I've enjoyed your broadcasts over the years."

"Well, this is very humbling, I must say." He finally took the ball and pen after establishing that it was really his autograph I wanted.

"This is very nice of you to ask me for this," he said.

It was beautiful to hear someone so famous and one of the best at his craft speak like that. This was no show he was putting on, and anybody who knew Ernie could tell you that this is really how humble he was. The fact that a kid would want his autograph, especially in a room full of ball players, was difficult for him to grasp.

"Here you go," he said, handing the ball back to me and shaking my hand.

"Thank you," I replied.

"No," he said. "Thank *you*."

Ernie died of cancer on May 4, 2010. His body lay in repose a couple of days later at Comerica Park in Detroit where more than 10,000 fans paid their respects. He is a member of the American Sportscasters Hall of Fame, the Michigan Sports Hall of Fame, the National Radio Hall of Fame, and the Baseball Hall of Fame. Our meeting was brief, but he is one of the nicest human beings I have ever met.

Bologna Sandwiches

The series with the Yankees was crazy. They came in only two games ahead of the Indians. The two teams would play four games in three days, including a double header on Friday to make up for the rainout in April, and they would draw more than 150,000 fans over the weekend.

The first game on Friday featured Phil Niekro pitching against Ron Guidry. The Yankees manufactured a run in the top of the first after Rickey Henderson got on base, and the Indians matched them in the bottom of the inning with a Joe Carter home run. The Yankees came back with two in the second on a two-run double by Don Mattingly, and the Indians matched them again that inning with an RBI double and RBI single from Brook Jacoby and Tony Bernazard, respectively.

The game remained tied until the bottom of the sixth when Julio Franco doubled in Pat Tabler. In the ninth inning, with the Indians up 4-3, Ernie Camacho came in to pitch for Niekro. With 65,000 fans holding their breaths, he got the Yankees out in order for the save.

The energy that game was similar to that of the Royals' game in May when 27,000 fans unexpectedly showed up to see the Indians win their eighth in a row, and the Twins' game when I was the batboy, and the Royals' Fourth of July game with more than 70,000 fans. The biggest difference, of course, was that this was in August against the Yankees, and the Indians were still in contention. It had been a long time since an August game meant something in Cleveland.

The second game that night was just as exciting. With the score tied, 3-3, in the ninth, Manager Pat Corrales elected to leave starter Tom Candiotti in the game. After Rickey Henderson was hit by a pitch and stole second, Don

159

The Ballboy

Mattingly launched a home run into the right field seats. The Indians had two on base in the bottom of the inning, but reliever Dave Righetti got Tony Bernazard to fly out to right field to end it.

As competitive and exciting as both of those games were, what stood out to me off the field was the Yankees' clubhouse between games. That was the first double header of the season, and I learned that both teams go to their clubhouses for about 20 minutes between games to rest and regroup. I wasn't planning to go up, but since I was hungry, I thought I'd see if they were serving any food. When I walked in, I saw a few players scarfing down bologna sandwiches to get something in their bodies, but not a word was spoken. All that could be heard was the sound of the players' cleats scraping the floor.

"Wow, you guys really blew that game!" I bellowed, breaking the awkward silence.

No I didn't. I wouldn't have lived to tell this story if I had.

Actually, realizing I was wearing an Indians' uniform behind enemy lines, I made myself a sandwich in about 10 seconds and bolted out, eating it on my way through the tunnel to the dugout. That was the first time I personally felt the intensity of the rivalry between these two teams. It had been years since both of them played each other this late in the season in a meaningful game. To lose a close one in front of a raucous crowd on the road did not sit well with the Yankees.

I found it interesting that in baseball, unlike sports such as basketball and football, there are rarely any pep talks in the clubhouse before or after games. A couple of teams had short meetings in the clubhouse before games after long losing streaks, meetings that I was not allowed to attend, but there was never a pregame or postgame speech from anyone and nothing between games of that doubleheader. I guess the celebrations after wins were satisfying enough, and the bologna sandwiches after losses said everything that needed to be said.

"Jackpot!"

The Tribe split the next two games with the Yankees, winning in 10 innings on Saturday, 6-5, and losing on Sunday, 12-8. They would fall to 6.5 games behind Boston with two months left. There was still time.

On Saturday, I spent a few minutes of batting practice in the outfield before coming into the dugout to mingle with the hitters and get them their bats. That's when I noticed a bat leaning against the wall below the bat rack. It had thick white tape around the barrel, signifying that it cracked at one time and was now strictly a batting practice bat. But, as I inspected it, the crack busted through the tape and stretched several inches from the top of the barrel to the middle, almost splitting the bat lengthwise.

With Carmen not down from the clubhouse yet, and since I was assisting the players, I declared the bat mine. I was going to immediately run it up to the laundry room, but I was anxious to see whose name was on it. I sat down next to one of the coaches on the bench and began to unravel it.

"Wow, that bat's seen better days," he said.

"Yeah, I haven't seen one crack through tape like this. I'm curious to see whose it is."

"It's kind of like scratching off a lottery ticket," he said.

I unraveled it carefully, one round at a time, to make sure that the bat hadn't already been sliced into two. After a few turns, I could feel that it was still in one piece and safe to continue. The amount of tape on this thing could have taped up a couple of ankles. Round and round I went, the bat getting thinner and thinner with the removal of each wrap. When I finally reached the end, the barrel of the bat with the player's name was facing the coach.

"Jackpot!" he said.

161

The Ballboy

I turned it my way. It said "Don Mattingly."

Mattingly was a six-time All-Star, 1984 AL batting champion, 1985 AL MVP, and 1985 Major League Player of the Year. He won nine Gold Glove awards at first base and three Silver Slugger awards in his 14-year career, finishing with 2,153 hits. He is another one who I and many believe should be in the Hall of Fame, but is not.

Fast forward a year to 1987…

I attended a game between the Indians and Yankees with a friend, and I brought my Mattingly bat. I assume you can't bring a bat into a game today, but it was a different world then. After the game we stood outside the clubhouse door waiting for the Yankees to come out when Don finally emerged. He was walking quickly; the bus was getting ready to leave.

"Mr. Mattingly," I said, extending the bat and a Sharpie marker. "Can you sign this please?"

He stopped and analyzed the bat. Then he looked at me. Then he looked at the bat again. As he was scribbling his name he looked up at me, then at the bat, then at me again. Obviously, he wanted to know how I got it, but I think he was afraid to ask because he felt like he should have known who I was. I talked to Don briefly during the 1986 season, and he was a very nice guy, but he wasn't someone I would have necessarily expected to remember me. When he handed me the bat and the marker, I let him off the hook.

"I was the ballboy here last year. You cracked this during batting practice."

"Oh, okay," he said, which I interpreted as, "Oh yeah, of course. Hey Bill, how have you been? I've missed having you around this season."

Some players from each team remembered my name when they returned their second time to the stadium in the 1986 season. And I do believe that some of them would have remembered me if I had worked again the next season. Would any of them remember me today? Nah. Maybe back then if I launched every warm-up throw over Dave Winfield's head, suggested to Billy Beane that he lose the attitude, or yelled at Kirk Gibson to get his own $%^&@#$ French fries, they would remember me. So, for obvious reasons, you can see why I'm fine that they don't.

Finding that Spark

The road trip following the Yankees' series featured four in Detroit, three in Baltimore, and three in New York. The Indians would lose all four to the Tigers, win all three against the Orioles, and lose all three to the Yankees. Though they were only 8.5 games back when they returned home, it felt worse than that because they dropped to sixth place. It was mid-August, and those seven losses to Detroit and New York were devastating. The pitching was too sporadic. In the three wins, the staff gave up a total of five runs. In the seven losses, they allowed at least six runs each game.

The Red Sox had a 3.5 game lead over the second-place Yankees, but the division title was still mathematically within reach for all seven teams. The Indians' next homestand would likely determine their season: 14 straight games, all against division rivals Baltimore, Milwaukee, Boston, and Toronto.

The series against Baltimore and the one against Milwaukee ended up fairly even. The Indians went 4-3 overall and dropped to 9.5 games behind Boston. They were still lingering, but this wasn't the time to linger; they had to make a move.

The most exciting part of those two series for me was the three-inning "Old Timers Game" prior to one of the Orioles' games. I met some former Indians greats like Bob Feller, Tito Francona, Max Alvis, and Sam McDowell, and some other former major leaguers like Brooks Robinson, Enos Slaughter, Gaylord Perry, and Joe Torre. I collected several autographs, though I didn't have much time to socialize with the guys since we had to get ready for the real game afterward.

One funny moment about that game was when Bob Feller gave me a ball and asked me to get him Joe Carter's autograph. Bob is widely considered the greatest player in Indians' history and one of baseball's greatest of all time. He won at least 24 games in each of the 1939, 1940, and 1941 seasons, spent the next three years fighting in World War II, then returned home and won at least 20 games in each of three more seasons. He was remarkable.

And not that Joe Carter wasn't remarkable in his own way, but for Bob to ask *him* for *his* autograph…

"Can you sign this, please?" I asked Joe as I handed him the ball from Bob.

"Sure."

I was going to leave it at that, but I wanted to see his reaction.

"It's for Bob Feller."

He stopped signing after "Joe."

"What?" he asked.

"He said he wanted your autograph."

"You're kidding, right?"

"Nope."

Joe shook his head, smiled, and finished signing. It was a very humble moment for him.

I enjoyed my time with all of the Orioles and Brewers players and coaches that second time around, and by no means was I getting bored with the job, but I was getting a little worn down. I certainly wasn't there just to collect a paycheck, but I was more grateful than I was early on that we were getting paid for what we were doing. I had a lot on my plate each day, and with the Indians looking like they were going to fall short of winning the division, the spark I needed wasn't igniting.

In the spring, I went to school during the day and worked this job at night. In the summer, I worked in my grandfather's rigging shop from about 7 A.M. to 3 P.M. and the Indians' job at nights and on weekends when the Indians were home, while also playing baseball and trying to spend time with my friends and family. And now, in August, my senior year was about to start. It was a lot.

Fortunately, that spark would finally ignite when the Red Sox returned to town, and it would stay lit for the rest of the season as some of the events that would transpire around me as ballboy from that point forward would be some of the best memories I would leave with. They would include my two favorite stories, which involved Wade Boggs, Jose Canseco, a digital watch, and a toilet.

"Can I Talk to Wade, Please?"

This isn't my favorite Wade Boggs story; that one is next. But this one gave me a good laugh.

We had a phone in the clubhouse. This was 1986, so nobody had a cell phone. There was one community wall phone inside the entrance door. It was generally used to receive calls from the Indians' clubhouse if they needed something, for us to call them if we needed something, or for players to make personal calls, though they rarely did. If they wanted to talk to family while on the road, they did so from their hotel rooms.

As I was heading out of the clubhouse and down to the field before the first game of the series, the phone rang, so I answered it.

"Clubhouse," I said.

"Is this the Red Sox clubhouse?" a kid probably about my age said on the other end, trying but failing to contain his excitement.

"Yes," I replied.

He cleared his throat to try to regain his composure.

"Can I talk to Wade, please?" he said in deeper voice.

"Who?" I asked.

"Wade Boggs."

Wade was standing near the television, about 15 feet from me.

"Who is this?" I asked.

"Uh...Steve."

"Does he know you?"

"Ye...Yes, he does," Steve said, clearly lying.

"Hang on."

167

As I brought the phone down from my ear, I could hear Steve and someone with him bubbling with enthusiasm, arguing about what to say if Wade got on the phone.

"Wade, it's for you, a guy named Steve," I said after covering the mouthpiece so Steve couldn't hear me. "I'm pretty sure it's a fan, unless you know a Steve who would call you here."

"I have no idea who that is," Wade said, waving his hand at me and turning away.

"I'm sorry," I said to Steve. "He's unavailable."

"Wait! Wait!" Steve cried out of desperation. "Is he there?"

"Yes, but he can't talk."

"Wait! Like…you can see him?"

"Of course," I said, having some fun. "He's right next to me."

Wade turned back to me and grinned.

"Oh my God!" he screamed "Please! Wade! Can you hear me! I love you Wade!"

Click.

I hung up on poor Steve, and Wade didn't hear him profess his love for him, though I applaud Steve for trying.

It's incredible how far technology has come. The clubhouse had one phone, no caller ID, and no voice mail. If it rang, our choices were to answer it or let it ring until the person on the other end decided to hang up, so we answered it. I assume Steve got through by calling the Indians' main office line and having them transfer him. There was no voice connection between us and the main office, so they couldn't tell us first that it was Steve for Wade; they just had to put it through. I'm surprised more fans didn't try that.

With that fun out of the way, I continued my trek down to the dugout, where I would witness one of the most bizarre baseball games ever, and a game in which I believe I was to blame for Wade Boggs, the league's best hitter, not getting a hit.

Seventeen After...

I went down to the dugout and sat near one of the Red Sox coaches. We talked about Greg Swindell, a pitcher for the Indians' AA minor league team, who was called up to pitch for the Indians that night. Greg, like Roger Clemens, attended the University of Texas and, like Roger, came with high expectations. He was the second pick that season in the draft. To bring a guy up from the minors to the big leagues his first season and straight from the AA level to face the best team in the league was a bold and unusual move, but Indians fans, including me, were excited to see what he could do.

The coach and I were chatting for a couple of minutes when Wade Boggs came down from the clubhouse. He walked straight over to me and handed me his digital watch.

"Here, can you tell me when it's 17 minutes past the hour?" he asked.

The game was at 7:35 P.M. It was now 7:03 P.M.

"Sure," I said. I didn't know why and I didn't ask; I was more interested in continuing my conversation with the coach, which I did as Wade walked to the other end of the dugout to stretch.

Wade was the game's best hitter. He came into that series hitting .351, on his way to hitting .357 for the season. He would accumulate 207 hits and would win his third batting title in four years (he would win two more in each of the next two seasons, giving him five in six years). He also led the league in walks in 1986 and hit with such precision that he rarely struck out.

Wade was a very superstitious person who followed the same routine each day, according to what I heard through media reports. Supposedly, he ate chicken before each game (though I didn't see it in the clubhouse, he may have done it at the hotel) and drew the Hebrew word "chai" (meaning "life")

169

in the dirt before each at-bat. I don't know how true either of those were, but there was another one I would later learn about that *was* true…and I was unwittingly right in the midst of it.

As I talked to the coach, I occasionally glanced at the watch…7:04…7:06…7:10…my glances became less frequent until I completely forgot to look. I was just so immersed in my conversation with the coach.

"Hey!" Wade shouted to me across the dugout. "What time is it?"

I looked at the watch. "Oh, it's 7:18," I said matter-of-factly.

He shot me a look like I just killed his dog. Visibly disgusted, he jogged onto the field without another word.

"He looked upset," I said to the coach. "Is 7:17 that big of a deal?"

"Yep," he said, not sugarcoating that I screwed up in a major way. "He always runs onto the field at 17 minutes after the hour that the game is going to start. Not a minute before and not a minute after…except for today."

He grinned at me after those last three words. I felt awful. Wade gave me one simple task, and I didn't do it. The stadium had a clock, but it was an analog clock that didn't have minute marks on it. Wade assumed a digital watch and a ballboy would solve that problem, but the battery in one of us went dead. When Wade returned from running, I gave him the watch and apologized. He mumbled that it was okay, but it wasn't.

Jump ahead to the game.

Wade, the leadoff hitter, grounded out to second base to start the game. The Indians would score once in the bottom of the inning to go up 1-0.

In the third inning, Wade grounded out to first base. The Red Sox scored three to take a 4-1 lead.

In the fourth inning, Wade flied out to left field. The Red Sox would score two more and go up 6-1. Greg Swindell's debut was finished.

In the sixth inning, the Indians' bullpen completely collapsed. The Red Sox scored a whopping 12 times to take an 18-1 lead. Wade batted twice in the inning. He grounded out to second the first time and walked the second time.

In the seventh inning, Wade popped out to the third baseman in foul territory. His night was finished. Dave Stapleton pinch hit for him in the eighth inning.

Seventeen After…

The Red Sox continued to show no mercy and would win the game, 24-5, in one of the biggest blowouts in baseball history. Marty Barrett went three for four. Jim Rice went three for four. Dwight Evans went three for four. Bill Buckner went five for six. Tony Armas went three for seven. Spike Owen went four for five. As a team, the Red Sox would crank out an astonishing 24 hits in 51 at-bats for an average of .471.

And what were the final numbers for Wade Boggs, the two-time batting champion who was about to win his third title?

No hits in five at-bats with a walk.

It would be only the second time the entire season in which he would have at least five at-bats and not get a hit, the other being opening day in Detroit more than four months earlier. It would be the only time all season in which he would have at least five at-bats as the leadoff hitter and not get a hit; he moved into the leadoff role with roughly 60 games left in the season.

In a 24-run, 24-hit barrage, and given all of those incredible hitting statistics on Wade that season and in past seasons, it didn't seem possible that he wouldn't get a hit that game…unless perhaps he relied on the ballboy to tell him the time.

171

It Was a Good Run

After the 24-5 debacle, the Indians would take two of the next three from Boston (like Boston's last trip to Cleveland, Roger Clemens did not pitch), and they would sit 9.5 games back with a 65-66 record. If the season wasn't finished yet, it was after the Toronto series. The Blue Jays swept the Indians, beating them 3-2, 6-3, and 9-1, and dropped them to 10.5 games out with a month to go and a 10-game road trip ahead. While the Blue Jays didn't mathematically knock out the Tribe, they mentally crushed them.

The Indians would go 5-5 on their road trip against Boston, Toronto, and Milwaukee and drop to 14 games back, essentially ending their run. They would come home to play for pride against California, Oakland, and Minnesota. I hoped that the Angels, who were likely going to win the West Division, would do it in Cleveland so that I could be there for the clubhouse celebration of spraying champagne all over each other, but they were still a few weeks away from clinching.

The Indians would lose two games to the Angels (the third game was rained out), including a 14-inning, five-hour affair on a school night, before playing three against the A's. Tony La Russa, who managed the White Sox earlier in the year, was now the manager of the A's. It was also September, which meant teams could expand their rosters to 40 players. The A's were out of the race and used that opportunity to call up players who had little or no Major League experience, guys like Terry Steinbach, Mike Gallego, and Mark McGwire, who would be the future of the team.

Carmen also decided to take off that weekend, making me the batboy for the entire series.

Pulling Excalibur from the Toilet

On Friday night, about a half hour before the start of the first game of the series with the A's, I was putting the bats and helmets in the racks. Jose Canseco, who was on his way to becoming the AL Rookie of the Year, was sitting on the bench by himself working on his brand new bat. By that, I mean he was like an artist engrossed in his next masterpiece.

Jose gripped the bat vertically at its midpoint with his left hand. The top of the barrel of the bat was resting on the bench between his legs. The handle was at eye level. Using his right hand, he meticulously rubbed a sticky substance on the handle, careful not to miss any spots. He was in a trance, oblivious to everyone and everything around him. When one of the coaches saw what he was doing, he sat down next to Jose and snapped him out of his spell.

"Hey, I don't think you can put that on there," the coach said to him.

"What are you talking about?" Jose replied.

"I think that's considered an illegal substance."

Jose was genuinely shocked. I don't know exactly what he was using or if it really was illegal, but coaches normally knew what they were talking about. It was a clear substance that looked similar to Stickum, which pro football players like Oakland Raiders' defensive back Lester Hayes used to help them catch the ball. I didn't know why that would have been illegal since players could use sticky pine tar, which was also Jose's argument.

After discussing it more with the coach, Jose stopped what he was doing and discarded the rest of the substance. He then walked over to me and extended his arms with the bat resting horizontally and loosely across both of his palms, as if he were presenting me with Excalibur, the legendary and magical sword of King Arthur.

"I need you to take good care of this," he said firmly, but politely. "I don't want it with the rest of the bats. Put it somewhere by itself."

"Sure," I said, gently taking it from his hands. There was a small gap between the top of the bat rack and the roof of the dugout. I carefully slid it in there, then turned to look at Jose for approval. He nodded.

"Thanks," he said.

Jose was batting third in the lineup. Since he would be batting in the top of the first, I took his bat down from atop the rack and had it ready for him as soon as Indians' pitcher Greg Swindell started his warm-up pitches.

Alfredo Griffin, the first batter in the inning, flew out to Joe Carter in right field. The next batter, Carney Lansford, grounded out to Julio Franco at second. Then Jose stepped up. It was easy to understand why his power stats were so impressive that season—he had 30 homers and 107 RBI coming into the game. The 22-year-old six-foot four-inch Cuban looked like he'd been chiseled from a hunk of granite. He had strength that I didn't see that season in a player his age.

Greg Swindell was a powerful rookie left-handed pitcher who squeezed in a victory after the disaster against Boston, but this showdown looked like man vs. boy. When Jose's bat connected with Greg's pitch, there was a collective gasp throughout the stadium.

"Holy $%^&!" one of the coaches yelled.

All of us in the dugout jumped up to the top of the steps to watch it fly. He hit it to left field, nearly halfway up the empty yellow seats in the upper deck. It was the longest home run I ever witnessed in that stadium. If the seats weren't there, the ball likely would have taken a few bounces on the ground and splashed into Lake Erie. I would bet if Greg were asked today about that pitch, one of thousands upon thousands he would throw in his 17-year major league career, he'd remember it. After the game, he told the media, "I just wanted to stand there and watch it myself." That's how far Jose hit it.

I hustled to retrieve the bat as Jose jogged around the bases, and I congratulated him as he crossed home plate. When I returned to the dugout, I inspected the bat. He hit it so hard and connected with it so cleanly that there were blue ink marks on it from the league's stamp on the baseball. I returned the bat to its special place on top of the bat rack, an honor the bat now earned.

With the A's down 4-1 entering the top of the fourth, Jose was the first man up, his second at-bat of the game. I had his bat ready for him when he came in from his position in left field. "Thanks, man," he said, almost as excited as I was to see what he and the bat would do for an encore.

But tragedy struck.

I don't know the location of the pitch Greg threw, but Jose didn't connect with it the way he'd expected. The ball popped up to the first base side and lazily fell into Pat Tabler's glove for the first out of the inning. But, just as I knew the home run in the first inning was going to be a home run the instant the ball connected with the bat, I knew by the sound of the pop up that something horrible happened. I ran to home plate to pick up the bat and saw what I feared. It was over.

"Did it crack?" Jose asked as we walked back together to the dugout.

"Yeah," I said somberly.

"$%^&!" Jose yelled as he ripped off his batting glove and flung it into the dugout.

As much as I felt bad for him, and as much as I hoped we might see a couple more home runs out of that bat, I now had a new mission: getting the bat from the dugout to my locker and to my home. I *had* to have that bat.

The game was only in the fourth inning. I couldn't leave the dugout and run it upstairs. Well, I probably could have taken a minute to sneak it up there when the A's were in the field, but what if Jose were to ask to see it for some reason? He loved that bat. He may have wanted to give it to a family member at the game or keep it for himself since it produced what was likely the longest home run of his young career. So, I leaned it against the wall underneath the bat rack where broken bats were kept during games, hoping it would still be there when the game was over.

As the game continued, so did the Indians' hitting attack. They scored two runs in the fourth and two more in the fifth, pushing the lead to 8-1. Tony La Russa was livid.

"You're nothing but a Triple A ballclub," he screamed at his players as he paced back and forth in the dugout. They *were* that in a sense, given all the minor leaguers they called up. But they also had a lot of veterans who weren't producing.

After the A's batted in the top of the sixth, I brushed off the dirt from the on-deck circle as I did each inning, then headed toward the other end of the dugout to go to the bathroom. The bathroom was as basic as could be. It had a sink and one toilet with a metal divider between them. The door was partially closed and the light was on. I started to walk toward it when the A's trainer, who was sitting on the steps at that end of the dugout, stopped me.

"Don't go in there," he said with a smirk. What was the smirk for? I thought he was messing with me, so I ignored his order and proceeded toward the bathroom.

"Don't go in there!" he said more emphatically, this time with a straight face.

"Why not?" I asked.

Bam! Bam! Bam! Bam! I jumped at the first *Bam!*

"I told you not to go in there," he said, laughing.

I looked across the dugout. Tony wasn't there. He had to be the one in the bathroom. And then...

Oh no!

I rushed toward the bat rack. There were no bats leaned against the wall below it.

Jose's bat! It's gone!

I tried to stay calm, hoping that maybe somebody moved it somewhere else. I searched high and low, trying to ignore the awful sounds coming from the bathroom that continued to ring through the dugout. I knew where the bat was, but I refused to believe it.

After a few minutes, Tony emerged from the bathroom without the bat. What did he do with it? I was so afraid of what I would find in there that I couldn't get myself to go in. I really had to go to the bathroom, but I held it for the rest of the game. The Indians won, 9-3.

The players cleared out of the dugout quickly, and it only took a few minutes for security to get the roughly 10,000 fans out of the stadium. The alternate ballboy who was helping me in the clubhouse that night grabbed the balls and water cooler.

"You can take that stuff up and start working on cleaning the cleats," I told him. "I'll be up in a minute." I wanted a moment alone to peek into the bathroom to see if any piece of the bat was salvageable. But, as he headed up, one of the clubhouse attendants came down.

"Where's the Canseco bat?" he asked anxiously. I was shocked.

"What are you talking about?" I said.

"I saw Canseco crack that bat early in the game. I want it." He'd been watching the game on TV in the clubhouse.

"It's gone," I said.

"What do you mean it's gone?"

I thought for a second about telling him what happened, but I really felt like I deserved the first shot at the bat.

"I set it aside after he cracked it, but about mid-game it was gone. I don't know what happened to it."

That wasn't a lie. I *assumed* it was Tony's weapon of choice in the bathroom, but I didn't know yet for sure.

"Aw, man," he said. He poked his head around to see if he could find it before going back up. He never looked in the bathroom because, well, why would a bat be in there? Convinced that it really was gone, he left.

Now by myself, I loaded the bats into the bat bag, carried it to the end of the dugout, and propped it against the wall outside the bathroom door. I slowly pushed open the door, as if I were about to encounter a murder scene. Fortunately, there were no dead bodies. And the sink was still there and intact. However, the divider between the sink and urinal took quite a beating. Tony probably could have come at it from the side and knocked it off the wall with a couple of swings. Instead, he hit the center of the narrow edge of it, over and over and over again.

But wait? Where is the bat?

I stepped around the divider to the toilet...

179

And there it was.

The barrel of the bat was submerged in the toilet water. Just the bat handle was sticking out. Incredibly, from what I could tell, the bat was still in one piece, which gives you an idea of the size and density of this piece of lumber. Tony destroyed that divider, and the bat held up through the torture.

Now came the big questions: Do I take a bat that has been sitting in the toilet? If so, how do I get it upstairs and home without that clubhouse attendant or anyone else seeing me with it? I stepped outside the bathroom and looked up the long tunnel; nobody was coming down. I went back in the bathroom and gently lifted the bat out of the water. As the water dripped onto the floor, I rotated it to see how much damage was done. The ink from the ball was still there, but there were now several gashes, compliments of Tony's swings.

How could I not take this? I thought. It was gross, but so what? Fortunately, whoever used the toilet before Tony went in there had flushed. I've sometimes wondered if I would have taken the bat if it were sitting in a pool of urine. Since it wasn't, I never have to answer that question.

I turned out the dugout lights and bathroom light, threw the bat bag over my shoulder, and dragged Canseco's bat along the carpet of the tunnel to help it dry before I got upstairs. When I reached the end of the tunnel, I had about 10 stairs to climb. At the top of those stairs was the laundry room with my duffel bag. A few feet from that was the entrance to the clubhouse. I left the bat bag at the foot of the stairs and ran Jose's bat into the laundry room, hiding it under my bag. I even took out my clothes and threw them on top for good measure. I went back down the steps to retrieve the bat bag, and then went into the clubhouse to finish my work for the night.

Sometimes a few of us would leave the clubhouse together to walk to our cars at the end of the evening, but on this night, I made sure to leave by myself and as soon as I could. When my chores were finished I went out the clubhouse door and into the laundry room, grabbed by stuff and the bat, and hustled out of there as quickly as I could.

It was quite a journey, but Excalibur was mine!

The Lost Story

One story from that night against the A's that often gets lost in my mind because of the Canseco bat story is that of catcher Terry Steinbach.

Terry played in the minors for four years and was called up to the majors in 1986 when the rosters were expanded. Once he finally made it to the big leagues, he never looked back. He became Oakland's starting catcher in 1987 and was instrumental in them getting to the World Series three straight times. Terry would play with the A's through 1996 before ending his career with three seasons in Minnesota. He would retire after the 1999 season with a career .271 average. He played in three All Star games and was the All Star Game MVP in 1988.

Terry started that Friday night game on the bench but replaced catcher Mickey Tettleton about halfway through. I didn't know who Terry was. I correctly assumed he was a minor leaguer who was called up that month, since I didn't remember him from the last time the A's were in town.

I handed Terry his bat to start the seventh inning; he was the leadoff hitter. There was nothing unusual about his approach, and nothing was said to him or about him by anyone in the dugout. With Greg Swindell still on the mound, Terry launched one over the wall—not nearly as far as Jose's a few innings earlier, but they all count the same once they fall over the fence. As Terry circled the bases, the dugout was going nuts, and I didn't know why. The Indians were still up 8-3.

I went out to pick up his bat and, as is customary for the batboy, I stayed out there to high-five him after he crossed home plate. Since there were no guys on base when Terry hit, I was the only one standing there waiting to congratulate him. As he approached the plate, I put up my right hand.

"Congratulations," I said.

With a glaze over his eyes and a smile as wide as home plate, Terry ignored my high-five stance and extended his right hand straight out.

"Thank you," he said to me sincerely, seemingly in awe of what he'd done, as he gave me a formal handshake.

When we got to the dugout, the players mobbed him. I finally figured out why he, his teammates, and the fans reacted the way they had: this was his first major league home run.

A couple of years later I was watching an A's game on television—sometime after Terry was named MVP of the All Star game and was quickly becoming one of the top catchers in the league—when the announcer talked about Terry's career. He noted that Terry did something that only about 60 players in the history of baseball did: he homered in his first major league at-bat.

I let that settle in my mind for a moment.

Wait a second! What did he say?

I did some research and, sure enough, on September 12, 1986, Terry Steinbach homered in his first major league at-bat against the Indians. So that wasn't just his first Major League home run, which was all I assumed when it happened, it was his first at-bat ever in the big leagues. I had no idea. Unfortunately, none of the articles on the game stated that I was the first to shake his hand after he crossed home plate, and I'm sure Terry won't remember me because he was so blinded by the stars in his eyes. But it was me.

Between the Canseco bat, Terry's homer, the Indians winning the game, and me getting to be batboy, that would be my most memorable game from beginning to end that season, which was now a few home games away from being finished. It was the perfect way to end my dream job.

"You Did Good"

After sweeping the A's and taking two of three from Minnesota, the Indians would go on a 13-game road trip to play Oakland, California, Seattle, and Minnesota (the earlier rainout at home against California would be made up on this trip). Mathematically, they weren't out of the race, but they were 15 games out with 16 to play. So, yeah, they were out. And so was pretty much everyone else. New York was in second place, 10 games behind Boston.

The Indians went 7-6 on the trip, then came home to play their last three games against Seattle. They swept that series to finish 84-78 and in fifth place, 11.5 games behind first-place Boston. It was the Indians' best season in nearly two decades and a bit of an anomaly, as it was sandwiched in between a 102-loss season in 1985 and a 101-loss season in 1987. I guess I picked the right year to win the job.

The 1986 season was special to the city of Cleveland for many reasons, primarily because it may have saved the team. At the start of that season people were talking about the possibility of the Indians moving. Tampa Bay was one city I'd heard mentioned a lot. But because of the winning streaks, staying in the pennant race for most of the season, and the general excitement the team brought night after night, an amazing thing happened: fans attended games!

Attendance in 1986 was 1.47 million, an average of about 18,000 a game. The year before it was 655,000, or 8,000 a game. In part, as a result of the attendance hike, the team was bought in December of 1986 by brothers David and Richard Jacobs, who would keep the team in Cleveland. Seven years later they would move into a brand new stadium known then as Jacobs Field, and today as Progressive Field. There is a wonderful article on that season and the

183

importance of it to the franchise by Jonathan Knight titled, "The Incredible Indians of '86." You can find it online; it's worth the read.

While the Indians wouldn't play in the postseason, it was fun to see two teams make it that I knew and liked. The Red Sox won the AL East with a 95-66 record. The Angels won the West at 92-70. In the NL, the Mets were the premier team with a 108-54 record in the East, while Houston finished at 96-66 in the West.

In the AL Championship Series, after trailing three games to one, the Red Sox stormed back to win it, four games to three. They advanced to the World Series to play New York, but the Mets would beat them in seven games. It was a memorable series for me, to be able to cheer for the guys I served that season. Once known to me from a distance as Rice, Boggs, Evans, Barrett, and Clemens, they were now Jim, Wade, Dwight, Marty, and Roger, guys I knew personally, even if for a short time…normal guys like me who happened to play ball for a living.

After the Indians' final series against Seattle, the goodbyes were as informal as the hellos were at the start of the season. Cy yelled at me for trying to take my uniform home—I honestly thought I could keep it—though he let me keep my hat, my windbreaker, and my heavy Starter jacket. Actually, he let me keep the hat and the windbreaker; the Starter jacket just happened to somehow get stuffed into my bag and thrown into my car. It meant more to me than it did to them given that I still have it today.

I was initially glad the season was over, especially since the Browns were into their season and playing like a Super Bowl contender, and the Cavs were about to start a new era with rookies they just drafted or traded for, including Brad Daugherty, Mark Price, and Ron Harper. But after a few weeks I did experience some withdrawal, and again the following spring when I knew Carmen was preparing for his second year on the job that I came so close to winning. But I had zero regrets. How could I after experiencing something so magical?

Billy worked me right to the last minute after that final game. When I thought I was finished and told him I was going to leave, he told me I wasn't because there were still towels in the training room to be cleaned up. Finally, after picking them up and when there was nothing left to be done, I walked over to him and shook his hand to say goodbye.

"Yeah, yeah, see you later," he said, quickly shaking my hand, which was about what I expected. But then he gave me the unexpected.

"Hey, dumb#$%," he said as I was walking out the door. He had an ever-so-slight smile.

"Thanks for all of your help. You did good."

Epilogue

In 2012, my wife and I, both huge fans of Bruce Springsteen's music, took our three sons to his concert in Louisville, Kentucky. The boys at the time were 15, 12, and nine years old. I took our 15-year-old to one of his concerts a couple of years earlier. It was the first Bruce experience for the other two.

About two hours into the show, while singing "Waitin' on a Sunny Day," Bruce brought our boys on stage to sing part of the chorus. They not only sang it, but they sang it well, thoroughly entertaining Bruce, the E Street Band, and the sold-out crowd of more than 17,000. The video of it has received tens of thousands of views on YouTube. If you'd like to watch it, search the terms "Springsteen Louisville Sunny Day."

After telling friends of ours what happened, one of them said to his wife, "Why do the Croyles always have lucky things like this happen to them?" I'm not sure specifically what other "lucky things" he was referring to, but his wife responded with the perfect answer, which was probably a slight and humorous jab at him: "Well, you have to get out and do things in order for lucky things to happen."

I've read a lot of quotes from famous people about "luck," and most of them have the same underlying theme: luck is our own creation. I shared one with you early in the book from Bruce Lee: "You have to create your own luck. You have to be aware of the opportunities around you and take advantage of them." McDonald's founder Ray Kroc said: "Luck is a dividend of sweat. The more you sweat, the luckier you get." General Douglas Macarthur said: "The best luck of all is the luck you make for yourself."

My wife and I saved our money for quite a while in order to be able to afford five general admission tickets for that concert, which would give us a chance to get into the pit right in front of the stage. We set aside time to try to buy the tickets online when they went on sale. Once we secured the tickets, we suggested to our boys that they make tee shirts to try to get Bruce's attention during the show. Our youngest wore one that said "Glory." Our middle son wore one that said "Days." Our oldest wore one that said "Please." Their hope was, of course, that he would play their favorite song, "Glory Days."

We got to Louisville several hours early to get in line, which was required if we wanted to be entered into a random drawing to have a chance at getting into the pit. About 300 people out of the 800 in line would be chosen. We were fortunate to have been five of the ones selected.

About five songs into the show, I put one son on my shoulders while my wife put another on hers. Bruce saw them from the stage between songs and said, "Glory! I like that!" referring to my youngest son's shirt. "I'm going to put you guys to work later." The seed was planted.

When Bruce started to sing "Waitin' on a Sunny Day" a couple of hours into the show, and knowing from reading about previous shows that Bruce often called kids on stage to sing it with him, I had my wife move as close to the stage with the boys as she could while I stayed a little ways back with the video recording on my phone. A couple of minutes into the song, I saw Bruce point at someone in the crowd and then point at his microphone, as if to say, "Do you want to come up and sing?" I didn't know to whom he was gesturing. A few seconds later, I saw our youngest son rise above the crowd. The other two boys followed, and the rest is history.

How much of that experience was luck? Earning and saving the money to buy the tickets wasn't luck. Getting through online to buy them may have required some luck, but we were ready at our computers, putting ourselves in the best position to get them. Making the tee shirts wasn't luck. Getting in line in time for the pit drawing wasn't luck. Having our number drawn to get into the pit was luck, but it wouldn't have happened if we weren't there on time to give ourselves a chance. And getting on stage may have required some luck, but we positioned our boys—putting them on our shoulders early in the show and getting close to the stage during the right song—to give them the best opportunity possible.

Epilogue

And yet, what most people say when they see the video or hear the story is, "Wow, you are so lucky," or as our friend said, "Why do the Croyles always have lucky things like this happen to them?" Maybe we were lucky, but as Bruce says in his song "Lucky Town," "When it comes to luck you make your own."

Like watching our boys perform with our favorite singer, my job with the Indians and Major League Baseball during the 1986 season was one of the greatest experiences of my life. It brought me tremendous joy to live through it then, and it still makes me happy to talk about it today. You already know what I went through to get the job. There was certainly some luck involved, but that luck wouldn't have materialized without my own effort.

Whatever you want to do, whether it involves work, school, a relationship, a team, a volunteer opportunity, a financial matter, or simply something fun, calculate the amount of risk you are willing to take and can safely take, and then go for it. You may need some luck along the way, but the harder you work toward making your desire come to fruition, the luckier you will likely be.

In the simplest terms, just remember what my mom said: "Anything is possible, but you'll never know unless you try."

Glossary of Players in the Book

Andy Allanson – Rookie catcher in 1986 with Cleveland; played for them through 1989. Had a .240 average in an eight-year career. Best year was in 1988 when he had 114 hits and 50 RBI.

Max Alvis – Two-time All-Star who played for nine years (1962-70), eight of them with Cleveland as a third baseman. Hit .247 with 111 home runs in his career.

Sparky Anderson – Managed Cincinnati from 1970-78 and Detroit from 1979-95. Had a career record of 2,194-1,834, was AL Manager of the Year twice, and won the World Series three times.

Tony Armas – Outfielder for 14 years with four teams. Two-time All-Star who hit 251 home runs, including 43 in 1984. Played for Boston in 1986, hitting .264 with 11 home runs in 121 games.

Scott Bailes – Rookie year was 1986 with Cleveland. Appeared in 62 games, starting 10 of them. Was 10-10 with seven saves. Played nine years for three teams, finishing 39-44 with 13 saves.

Harold Baines – Outfielder and designated hitter for 22 years with five teams, had 2,866 hits, and a lifetime average of .289. Hit .296 in 1986 for the Chicago White Sox and played in six All-Star games. Elected to the Hall of Fame in 2019.

Dusty Baker – Outfielder for 19 years with four teams. Two-time All-Star. Won the World Series with the Los Angeles Dodgers in 1981. His last year was with Oakland in 1986 as a part-time player. He would later manage the San Francisco Giants, Chicago Cubs, Cincinnati, and Washington.

Steve Balboni – Played for 11 years with four teams, including Kansas City from 1984-88. A first baseman, he hit 181 home runs in his career, including 29 in 1986.

George Bamberger – Managed Milwaukee for five years and the New York Mets for two years. Overall record was 458-478. Twice managed Milwaukee to more than 90 wins, but they didn't make the playoffs either year.

Jesse Barfield – Two-time Gold Glove winner had one of the best outfield arms in baseball. Hit 241 home runs in 12 years with Toronto and the New York Yankees. Best season was with Toronto in 1986 when he had 40 home runs and 108 RBI, won the Silver Slugger Award, and was selected to his only All-Star game.

Marty Barrett – Played second base in a 10-year career, nine with Boston. Had his best overall year in 1986 when he hit .286 with 179 hits (including 39 doubles), 60 RBI, and 15 stolen bases.

Billy Beane – Outfielder who played for four teams from 1984-89, including for Minnesota in 1986. Was named head of baseball operations for Oakland in 1997 and has been instrumental in the team's success since then.

George Bell – Outfielder who played 12 years, nine with Toronto. Had 265 home runs and 1,002 RBI, including a combined 78 home runs and 242 RBI in the 1986 and 1987 seasons.

Tony Bernazard – Second baseman for Cleveland from 1984-87; played for 10 years overall. Had a career .262 average; best year was 1986 when he hit .301.

Bert Blyleven – Pitched for 22 years for five teams. Won 287 games, had a 3.31 ERA, was a two-time All-Star, and was elected to the Hall of Fame in 2011. In 1986 with Minnesota, he was 17-14 with a 4.01 ERA.

Wade Boggs – Third baseman who played for 18 years with Boston, the New York Yankees, and Tampa Bay. Had a career .328 average, played in 12 All-Star games, won five batting titles (1983 and 1985-88), and was elected to the Hall of Fame in 2005. Played for Boston in 1986; won his third batting title that year with a .357 average.

Bobby Bonds – Father of former player Barry Bonds, the outfielder played 14 years with eight teams from 1968-81. Hit .268 with 332 home runs. Served as Cleveland's hitting coach in 1986.

Bob Boone – Catcher for 19 years with three teams. Four-time All-Star and a World Series champion with Philadelphia in 1980. In 1986 with California, he hit .222. He hit .254 for his career.

Dennis "Oil Can" Boyd – At just 155 pounds, he pitched 10 years with three teams and won 78 games. Recorded his most wins in 1986 when he went 16-10 for Boston.

George Brett – Hit .305 in a 21-year career, all with the Kansas City. Hit .290 in 1986. Best season was .390 in 1980. Played in 13 All-Star games, won three batting titles, and was the 1980 Major League Player of the Year. Played third base and was elected into the Baseball Hall of Fame in 1999 with 98.2 percent of the vote.

Bill Buckner – Played primarily first base for five teams in 22 years, winning the NL batting title in 1980 with the Chicago Cubs. Finished his career with a .289 average and 2,715 hits. Hit .267 with 168 hits for Boston in 1986.

Brett Butler – Center fielder who played for 17 years. Was with Cleveland from 1984-87 and stole 164 bases in that time. In 1986, he hit .278, had 32 steals, and led the AL in triples with 14.

Ernie Camacho – Pitched for six teams in 10 years, half of those years with Cleveland. Appeared in 51 games in 1986, finishing 2-4 with 20 saves.

Bill Campbell – Relief pitcher for seven teams in 15 years. He was 83-68 with 126 saves in his career. He was 3-6 with a 3.88 ERA and three saves for Detroit in 1986.

Tom Candiotti – Knuckleball pitcher who played for Cleveland from 1986 through part of 1991, and again in 1999, his final season after 16 years in the big leagues. Won 16 games and pitched a career-high 17 complete games in 1986.

John Cangelosi – Rookie outfielder with the Chicago White Sox in 1986; played for 13 years with seven teams. Had a career batting average of .250. Had 50 stolen bases in 1986.

Jose Canseco – AL Rookie of the Year in 1986 with Oakland; played on their World Series teams from 1988-90. Hit 462 home runs with six different teams in 17 years. The outfielder played in six All-Star games and won the AL MVP Award in 1988.

Rod Carew – An infielder who played for 19 years with Minnesota and California, retiring in 1985. Had 3,053 hits and batted .328. Played in 18 All-Star games and won seven batting titles. Elected to the Hall of Fame in 1991.

Joe Carter – Outfielder and first baseman who played for 16 years, including with Cleveland from 1984-89. Had 29 home runs and 121 RBI in 1986 and finished ninth that year in the AL MVP voting.

Rick Cerone – Played for 18 years with eight teams, hitting .245 lifetime. Was a backup catcher for most of his career, including in 1986 with Milwaukee.

Aroldis Chapman – Started his career with Cincinnati in 2010 and was still pitching in 2019 with the New York Yankees. The six-time All-Star recorded the fastest pitch in Major League Baseball history at 105.1 miles per hour.

Joe Charboneau – Played three seasons, all with Cleveland, before injuries ended his career. The outfielder was the 1980 AL Rookie of the Year with a .289 batting average, 23 home runs, and 87 RBI.

Roger Clemens – Pitched for 24 years with Boston, the New York Yankees, Toronto, and Houston. Won 354 games, including 24 in 1986 with Boston. Alleged ties to steroid use have kept him out of the Hall of Fame.

Dave Collins – Infielder and outfielder who played for eight teams in 16 years. Hit .270 with 27 stolen bases for Detroit in 1986.

Billy Consolo – Coach for Detroit under Sparky Anderson for 14 seasons, including in 1986. Played for 10 years from 1953-62.

Cecil Cooper – First baseman for Milwaukee for 11 years after playing for Boston from 1971-76. Had 2,192 hits, 241 home runs, a .298 average, and was a five-time All-Star.

Pat Corrales – Managed four teams, including Cleveland from 1983-87. His best year was with Philadelphia in 1982 (89-73). His second best was with Cleveland in 1986 (84-78).

Doug DeCinces – Played third base for three teams in 15 years. Hit 237 home runs and was an All-Star in 1983. Hit .256 with 26 home runs and 96 RBI with California in 1986.

Rob Deer – Played for 11 years with five teams, mainly as an outfielder. Hit .220 with 230 home runs during his career, including 21 or more for eight consecutive seasons. For Milwaukee in 1986, he had career highs in home runs (33) and RBI (86).

Rick Dempsey – A catcher who played for 24 years with seven different teams, half of them with Baltimore from 1976-86 and in 1992. Was the 1983 World Series MVP.

Joe DiMaggio – The center fielder played for the New York Yankees from 1936-1951. Was a 13-time All-Star, won two batting titles, was the AL MVP three times, and was the Major League Player of the Year in 1939. Elected to the Hall of Fame in 1955.

Ken Dixon – Pitched for Baltimore from 1984-87, finishing with a 26-28 record. Won 11 of those games in 1986.

Brian Downing – Outfielder and catcher for 20 years with three teams. Had 2,099 hits and 275 home runs. In 1986 with California, he had 20 home runs and 95 RBI. He was an All-Star in 1979.

Don Drysdale – A pitcher for the Brooklyn Dodgers and Los Angeles Dodgers from 1956-69, he finished with a record of 209-166, a 2.95 ERA, and 167 complete games. Nine-time All-Star, 1962 Cy Young Award winner, 1962 Major League Player of the Year, and elected to the Hall of Fame in 1984.

Darrell Evans – First and third baseman who played for 21 years. Hit 414 home runs, including 136 of them in his last five years from 1985-89. Led the AL in home runs with 40 in 1985; hit 29 more in 1986. Played with Detroit from 1984-88.

Dwight Evans – Right fielder for most of his career. Played for 19 years with Boston and his final year in 1991 with Baltimore. Hit .272 for his career with 385 home runs and 2,446 hits. Was a three-time All-Star and won eight Gold Gloves. Hit 26 home runs and 97 RBI in 1986.

Bob Feller – Played all 18 seasons with Cleveland. Won 266 games, played in eight All-Star games, and was the 1940 Major League Player of the

Year. Threw three no-hitters and 12 one-hitters during his career. Elected to the Hall of Fame in 1962.

Carlton Fisk – Catcher for 24 years with Boston and the Chicago White Sox; finished with 376 home runs. An 11-time All-Star and the 1972 AL Rookie of the Year. Had 14 home runs and 63 RBI in 1986 with Chicago. Elected in 2000 to the Hall of Fame.

Mike Flanagan – Pitched for 18 years, 15 of them with Baltimore. Finished with a record of 167-143. Was 7-11 in 1986. His best year was in 1979 when he won 23 games.

Julio Franco – Played for 23 years. Was with Cleveland from 1983-88, 1996, and part of 1997, primarily as the shortstop. Had a career .298 average and stole 30 or more bases in each of four seasons. In 1986, he hit .306 with 183 hits.

Tito Francona – Father of Cleveland manager Terry Francona, Tito played for nine teams in 15 years (1956-70), six of them with Cleveland. The outfielder and first baseman hit 272 with 125 home runs and 656 RBI. Was an All-Star in 1961.

Mike Gallego – Played shortstop, second base, and third base in a 13-year career with three teams, and was with Oakland for their three World Series appearances from 1988-90. In 1986, he hit .270 in 20 games after being called up from the minor leagues in September.

Lou Gehrig – Played first base for the New York Yankees from 1923-39. Batted .340 lifetime, played in seven All-Star games, won the Triple Crown in 1934, won six World Series, and was elected to the Hall of Fame in 1939 by special election due to a fatal disease that would claim his life two years later.

Kirk Gibson – Played for 17 years. Was an outfielder with Detroit from 1979-87 and 1993-95. Would later manage Arizona. In 1986, he hit .268 with 28 home runs, 86 RBI, and 34 steals.

Alex Grammas – Third base coach for Detroit from 1980-91. Played for 10 years from 1954-63, and he was the Milwaukee manager for a couple of seasons in the 1970s.

Pumpsie Green – First black player for Boston; played with them from 1959-62 before ending his career in 1963 with the New York Mets. Hit .246 lifetime and played second base and shortstop.

Bobby Grich – Infielder for 17 years with California and Baltimore. Six-time All-Star and four-time Gold Glove winner at second base. Hit .268 in 98 games with California in his final year in 1986.

Ken Griffey, Sr. – Father of Ken Griffey Jr., and a member of Cincinnati's "Big Red Machine" in the 1970s. An outfielder, he played for 19 years, including with the New York Yankees from 1982-86. Was hitting .303 when he was traded in the middle of the 1986 season to Atlanta.

Alfredo Griffin – The 1979 AL Rookie of the Year with Toronto and was an All-Star in 1984. Played shortstop for 18 years with four teams. Hit .285 in 1986 with 33 stolen bases for Oakland.

Ron Guidry – Four-time All-Star who won two World Series and pitched all 14 years of his career with the New York Yankees. Was the 1978 Major League Player of the Year and the 1978 Cy Young Award winner. Won 22 games in 1985. Went 9-12 in 1986. Retired after the 1988 season.

Ozzie Guillen – Shortstop for 16 years, including 13 with the Chicago White Sox from 1985-97. Was the 1985 AL Rookie of the Year. In 1986, he hit .250. Would become a manager for the Chicago White Sox. Won the AL Manager of the Year Award in 2005 when they won the World Series.

Mel Hall – He was with Cleveland from 1984-88. The outfielder had a .276 career average and hit .296 in 1986.

Toby Harrah – Shortstop, third baseman, and second baseman for three teams in 17 years, with 1986 being his last year. Played in four All-Star games and hit .264 lifetime.

Mickey Hatcher – Played outfield for Minnesota in 1986 and hit .278 that year. Had a 12-year career with Minnesota and the Los Angeles Dodgers, hitting .280 overall.

Neal Heaton – Pitched for 12 years with seven different teams. Was 3-6 with Cleveland in 1986 before being traded in June of that season to Minnesota.

Rickey Henderson – A career .297 hitter, the left fielder was elected to the Hall of Fame in 2009. Stole 1,406 bases, including 100 or more three times. Stole 87 for the New York Yankees in 1986. Played in 10 All-Star games in a 25-year career with nine different teams.

Larry Herndon – The outfielder played for 14 years, including the last seven with Detroit from 1982-88. Hit .274 for his career.

Charlie Hough – Knuckleball pitcher who played for 25 years with four teams, including with Texas from 1980-90. Was 17-10 in 1986 and named to the All-Star team. Finished his career with an even record of 216 wins and 216 losses.

Dick Howser – Managed the New York Yankees for a couple of seasons before managing Kansas City from 1981-86, winning the World Series in 1985. Overall record was 507-425. Came in second twice for the AL Manager of the Year Award, in 1984 and 1985.

Kent Hrbek – First baseman for Minnesota his entire 14-year career. Was in the 1982 All-Star game and won the World Series twice. Hit 20 or more home runs in each of 10 seasons and hit 293 in his career. Hit 29 home runs and 91 RBI in 1986.

Bruce Hurst – In 15 years pitching with four teams, he finished with a 145-113 career record. In 1986 with Boston, he was 13-8 with a 2.99 ERA.

Pete Incaviglia – Outfielder for six teams in 12 years. His rookie year was in 1986 with Texas. Had 30 home runs and 88 RBI that season.

Reggie Jackson – Played right field in a 21-year career with Oakland, Baltimore, the New York Yankees, and California. Was 40 years old and with California in 1986, the second-last year of his career, when he hit 18 home runs. Finished with 563 home runs and 1,702 RBI. He was elected to the Hall of Fame in 1993.

Brook Jacoby – Played third base for Cleveland from 1984-90 and had a career average of .270. Was a two-time All-Star, including in 1986 when he hit .288 with 17 home runs and 80 RBI.

Cliff Johnson – Designated hitter and first baseman. Played for seven teams in 15 years. Played in an average of less than 100 games a season (he was often used as a pinch hitter). His last year was in 1986 with Toronto when he hit 15 home runs in 107 games.

Wally Joyner – First baseman for 16 years with four teams. Only All-Star game was his rookie year in 1986 with California when he hit .290 with 22 home runs and 100 RBI. Finished second in the AL Rookie of the Year voting to Jose Canseco.

Jim Kern – Pitched for six teams in 13 years, including with Cleveland from 1974-78 and in 1986. Finished with a career record of 53-57 with 88 saves.

Dave Kingman – Infielder and outfielder for seven teams in 16 years. Hit 442 home runs in his career. Had 35 home runs and 94 RBI with Oakland in 1986, his final season.

Duane Kuiper – Played second base for Cleveland from 1974-81 and the Giants from 1982-85. Lifetime average of .271. Hit just one home run in his career, with Cleveland in 1977.

Tony La Russa – Managed the Chicago White Sox in 1986, was fired during the season, and was hired by Oakland that same year. Managed 33 years overall, had a 2,728-2,365 record, and won the World Series three times (with Oakland in 1989 and with St. Louis in 2006 and 2011).

Pete Ladd – Pitched for three teams in six seasons. His last year was with Seattle in 1986 when he went 8-6 with six saves in 52 relief appearances.

Carney Lansford – Primarily a third baseman for 15 years with three teams, including with Oakland from 1983-92. Was an All-Star in 1988. In 1986 with Oakland, he hit .284 with 19 home runs and 72 RBI.

Chet Lemon – Outfielder for 16 years with the Chicago White Sox and Detroit. Was with Detroit in 1986 and hit .251. Played in three All-Star games and had a career average of .273 with 1,875 hits.

Fred Lynn – Center fielder with Baltimore from 1985-88. Played 17 years overall. Hit .283, played in nine All-Star games, was the 1975 AL Rookie of the Year and MVP, and won the 1979 AL batting title. In 1986, he hit .287 with 23 home runs.

Mickey Mantle – A career .298 hitter with 536 home runs from 1951-68 with the New York Yankees, he was elected to the Hall of Fame in 1974. The outfielder was a three-time AL MVP, 1956 AL Triple Crown winner, and played in 20 All-Star games.

Billy Martin – Managed five teams. Known mostly for his stints as manager of the New York Yankees where he was hired, fired, hired, fired, hired, fired, hired, fired, hired, and fired over 14 years. He won the World Series with New York in 1977.

Dennis Martinez – Pitcher for Baltimore from 1976 through part of 1986, he would win 245 games in his career with a 3.70 ERA. Was traded in June of 1986 to Montreal.

Mike Mason – Was 29-39 pitching for seven seasons with three teams. With Texas in 1986, he posted his best record at 7-3.

Don Mattingly – First baseman who played for 14 years, all with the New York Yankees. Hit .307 lifetime, played in six All-Star games, was the 1985 Major League Player of the Year, and won the 1984 AL batting title. In 1986, he hit .352 (second behind Wade Boggs) and led the league in hits (238) and doubles (53).

Sam McDowell – Pitched for 15 years (1961-75) with four teams, 11 of those years with Cleveland. Career record was 141-134. Was a six-time All-Star and won the AL ERA title (2.18) in 1965.

Mark McGwire – Played for 16 years with Oakland and St. Louis as a first baseman. Was a 12-time All-Star and the 1987 AL Rookie of the Year. Was part of Oakland's World Series teams from 1988-90. In 1986, he was called up from the minors in September and played 18 games, batting .189 with three home runs.

John McNamara – Managed six teams in 19 years, including Boston in 1986 when he led them to the World Series. Finished his career with a record of 1,160-1,233.

Hal McRae – Played for 19 years, 15 with Kansas City. Was a designated hitter and outfielder who hit .290 lifetime and played in three All-Star games. Hit .252 in 1986, his second-last season.

Paul Molitor – Third baseman for 21 years with three teams, including 15 with Milwaukee. Was a seven-time All-Star, the 1993 World Series MVP, had 3,319 hits, and was elected to the Hall of Fame in 2004. In 1986 with Milwaukee, he hit .281. Career average was .306.

Sid Monge – Pitched for five teams in 10 years, including with Cleveland from 1977-81. Finished with a career record of 49-40 with 56 saves.

Jack Morris – Pitched for 18 years, including with Detroit from 1977-90. Pitched in five All-Star games and was the 1991 World Series MVP with Minnesota. Finished with a career record of 254-186. In 1986, he was 21-8.

Lloyd Moseby – Center fielder for 12 years, including 10 with Toronto. All-Star in 1986. Hit .253 that season with 149 hits, 21 home runs, and 86 RBI.

Eddie Murray – Played for 21 years, including with Baltimore from 1977-88 and in 1996. Hit .287 with 504 home runs in his career. Hit .305 in 1986. Played first base. Elected into the Hall of Fame in 2003.

Tony Muser – Played first base and outfield for nine years for four teams, managed Kansas City for six years, and was the third base coach for Milwaukee from 1985-88.

Joe Niekro – Brother of pitcher Phil Niekro. Pitched for the New York Yankees in 1986 and went 9-10. Played for 22 years with seven teams. Finished his career with a record of 221-204.

Phil Niekro – The knuckleballer pitched for 24 years, mostly with Atlanta. Joined Cleveland in 1986 at the age of 47. Went 11-11 that year and 7-11 in 1987 before going to Toronto later that season. Won 318 games and was elected to the Hall of Fame in 1997.

Al Nipper – Pitched seven years for three teams. In 1986 with Boston, he was 10-12 in 26 starts with three complete games.

Otis Nixon – Played outfield for 17 years, four of them with Cleveland from 1984-87. Stole 620 bases in his career, including a high of 72 in 1991 for Atlanta. In 1986, he hit .263 and stole 23 bases.

Dickie Noles – Pitched for six teams in 11 years. Was 3-2 in 32 relief appearances for Cleveland in 1986.

Bryan Oelkers – Pitched just two years, in 1983 with Minnesota and 1986 with Cleveland. Appeared in 35 games for Cleveland, most of them in relief, going 3-3 with one save.

Ben Oglive – Left fielder for 16 years with three teams. Three-time All-Star who had 235 home runs in his career. His last year was in 1986 with Milwaukee, when he hit .283 in 103 games.

Spike Owen – Infielder for 13 years with five teams. In 1986, he played for both Seattle and Boston. Hit .231 that year and .246 for his career.

Lance Parrish – Catcher for 19 seasons, including 10 with Detroit from 1977-86. Hit 20 or more home runs in seven seasons and won three Gold Glove awards. Eight-time All-Star, including in 1986 when he hit 22 home runs.

Gaylord Perry – Won 314 games in a 22-year career with eight teams from 1962-83. Threw 303 complete games and had a 3.11 ERA. Was a five-time All-Star, two-time Cy Young Award winner (one in each league), and was elected to the Hall of Fame in 1991.

Lou Piniella – Managed the New York Yankees from 1986-88 after playing for them for 11 years. Managed Cincinnati to the World Series championship in 1990.

Jim Presley – Primarily a third baseman who played for eight years with three teams. Best season was in 1986 with Seattle when he hit .265 with 27 home runs, 107 RBI, four triples, and was selected to the All-Star team.

Kirby Puckett – Center fielder for Minnesota from 1984-95. Was a 10-time All-Star, won one batting title, was the MVP of the 1991 AL Championship Series, won the World Series twice, hit .318 lifetime, and was elected to the Hall of Fame in 2001. Hit .328 with 31 home runs and 96 RBI in 1986. He died in 2006 at the age of 45 after suffering a stroke.

Dan Quisenberry – Relief pitcher with Kansas City from 1979-1988. Had 244 career saves and was the AL Rolaids Relief Pitcher of the Year in 1980 and 1982-85. Appeared in three All-Star games.

Willie Randolph – Six-time All-Star second baseman who played 18 years, including 13 with the New York Yankees from 1976-88. Won two World Series with New York.

Harold Reynolds – Two-time All-Star and three time Gold Glove second baseman for three teams in 12 years. Stole 250 bases in his career, including 30 in 1986 and 60 in 1987 with Seattle.

Jim Rice – The left fielder played his entire 16-year career with Boston. Hit .324 in 1986. Hit 39 home runs in 1977, 1979, and 1983, and 46 home runs in 1978 (he also won the AL MVP that year). Elected to the Hall of Fame in 2009.

Dave Righetti – Pitched for 16 years with five teams, including his first 11 with the New York Yankees. Was the AL Rookie of the Year in 1981 and the AL Rolaids Relief winner in 1986 and 1987. Recorded a career high 46 saves in 1986. Had 252 saves overall.

Jose Rijo – The 1990 World Series MVP for Cincinnati and an All-Star in 1994. Pitched for 14 years with three teams, including Oakland from 1985-87. Was 9-11 in 1986 with a 4.65 ERA.

Cal Ripken, Jr. – Shortstop who played in 3,001 games in 21 years, all with Baltimore. Played in a record 2,632 consecutive games. Was in 19 All-Star games. Was the 1982 AL Rookie of the Year and the 1983 and 1991 Major League Player of the Year. Elected to the Hall of Fame with 98.5 percent of the vote in 2007. In 1986, he hit .282 with 25 home runs and 81 RBI.

Brooks Robinson – Played 23 years, from 1955-77, all of them with Baltimore at third base. Played in 18 All-Star games, was the AL MVP in 1964, the World Series MVP in 1970, and was elected to the Hall of Fame in 1983.

Frank Robinson – Was a coach for Baltimore in 1986. Played for 21 years with five teams. Hit .294 and had 2,943 hits, 586 home runs, and 1,812 RBI. Played in 14 All-Star games, won the MVP award in both leagues, and was the 1956 NL Rookie of the Year, the 1966 AL Triple Crown winner, and the 1966 AL batting champion. Elected to the Hall of Fame in 1982.

Babe Ruth – Played for 22 years, 15 with the New York Yankees. Hit 714 home runs, was the AL home run champion 12 times, and won the World Series seven times.

Bret Saberhagen – Pitched for 16 years, including with Kansas City from 1984-91. Went 20-6 in 1985 and 23-6 in 1989. He won the Cy Young Award both of those years, and he was the World Series MVP in 1985. Went 7-12 in 1986.

Ken Schrom – Pitched for seven years, the last two with Cleveland in 1986 and 1987. Was 14-7 in 1986 with a 4.54 ERA.

Don Schulze – Pitched for six years with five different teams, half of those years with Cleveland. Was 4-4 with a 5.00 ERA in 1986.

Herb Score – Pitched for Cleveland from 1955-59 and for the Chicago White Sox from 1960-62. Was the 1955 AL Rookie of the Year. Broadcasted Cleveland games for 34 years.

Ruben Sierra – An outfielder and four-time All-Star in 20 years with nine teams. Hit 306 home runs and drove in 1,322 runs. In his rookie year in 1986, at 20 years old, he had 101 hits and 16 home runs in 113 games.

Enos Slaughter – Played outfield for 19 years in the '30s, '40s, and '50s for four teams. Was a 10-time All-Star who hit .300 and had 2,383 hits. Elected to the Hall of Fame in 1985.

Lonnie Smith – Left fielder who played with six teams in 17 years. Hit .287 with 146 hits for Kansas City in 1986. Won the World Series three times with three different teams.

Cory Snyder – Hit .272 with 24 home runs in 1986 with Cleveland, his rookie season. Finished fourth in the AL Rookie of the Year voting. Played right field and shortstop. Was with the Indians through 1990 and in the majors through 1994.

Dave Stapleton – Infielder for seven years with Boston. Finished second in the AL Rookie of the Year voting in 1980. Ended his career after the 1986 season and finished with a lifetime .271 average.

Terry Steinbach – Played for 14 years with Oakland and Minnesota as a catcher and first baseman. Named to three All-Star games, was the MVP in the 1988 game, and was on Oakland's three World Series teams from 1988-90. In 1986, he was called up from the minors in September; played in six games and batted .333.

Dave Stewart – An All-Star and the World Series MVP with Oakland in 1989. Pitched for 16 years with five teams. In 1986 with Oakland, he was 9-5 with a 3.74 ERA.

Dave Stieb – Seven-time All-Star pitcher in 16 years, 15 of them with Toronto. Finished with a record of 176-137. Had at least 11 wins in each of 10 seasons. Finished 7-12 with a 4.74 ERA in 1986.

Jim Sundberg – Won six Gold Gloves as a catcher in 16 years and played in three All-Star games. Spent most of his career with Texas. Played for Kansas City in 1985 and 1986.

Greg Swindell – Pitched for six teams in 17 years, finishing with a 123-122 record. Pitched his first six years with Cleveland. Was drafted by Cleveland with the second pick in the 1986 draft and was brought up later that season from the team's AA minor league club. Was 5-2 in 1986.

Pat Tabler – Played primarily first base for Cleveland from 1983-88 before being traded to Kansas City during the 1988 season. Played for 12 years. Best season at the plate was in 1986 when he hit .326, the fourth best average in the AL.

Frank Tanana – Won 240 games in 21 years with six teams. Was 12-9 in 1986 with Detroit. Had the lowest ERA in the AL at 2.54 in 1977 with California.

Danny Tartabull – An All-Star in 1991 who played for 14 years with six teams. Rookie year was in 1986 with Seattle when he hit .270 with 25 home runs and 96 RBI, good for fifth in the AL Rookie of the Year voting. Hit 262 home runs in his career. Was a designated hitter and outfielder.

Walt Terrell – A pitcher for Detroit from 1985-88, he played 11 years overall. Lifetime record of 111-124. In 1986, he was 15-12.

Mickey Tettleton – A catcher, outfielder, and first baseman. Played for four teams in 14 years. Was a two-time All-Star and won three Silver Slugger awards. Hit 245 home runs in his career, including four seasons of 31 or more. Played for Oakland in 1986; hit 10 home runs in 90 games.

Andre Thornton – Played first base and was a designated hitter for Cleveland from 1977-87. Played 14 years overall and hit 253 home runs, including 22 or more in each of six seasons. Had 17 home runs and 66 RBI in 1986.

Jeff Torborg – Managed Cleveland for three years in the 1970s. Also managed the Chicago White Sox, New York Mets, Montreal, and Florida. Was the bullpen coach for the New York Yankees in 1986.

Joe Torre – Played from 1960-77 with three teams as a catcher, first baseman, and third baseman. Was a nine-time All-Star, hit .297 for his career, was the Major League Player of the Year and batting champion in 1971, was the AL Manager of the Year with the New York Yankees in 1996 and 1998, and was elected to the Hall of Fame in 2014.

Jim Traber – First baseman and outfielder for Baltimore. Played four major league seasons, hitting .227 with 27 home runs. Best year was 1986 when he hit .255 with 13 home runs.

Alan Trammell – Played shortstop for 20 years, all with Detroit. Hit .285 for his career. In 1986, he hit .277 with 21 home runs and 25 stolen bases. Elected to the Hall of Fame in 2018.

Mike Trout – Began his career with the Los Angeles Angels in 2011 and was still playing for them in 2020. Considered one of the best players in the game. Through 2019, the center fielder was an eight-time All-Star, seven-time winner of the Silver Slugger Award, and three-time AL MVP.

Willie Upshaw – First baseman and outfielder. Played for 10 years, nine of them with Toronto and his last one with Cleveland in 1988. Best season was in 1983 when he had 177 hits, 27 home runs, and 104 RBI. In 1986, he hit .251 with nine home runs and 60 RBI.

Tom Veryzer – The shortstop played for four teams in 12 years from 1973-84, including with Cleveland from 1978-81. Hit .241 for his career.

Earl Weaver – Managed Baltimore from 1968-82 before retiring. Came out of retirement to manage the team in 1985 and 1986 before leaving for good. His record was 1,480-1,060. Won the World Series in 1970. Elected to the Hall of Fame in 1996.

Lou Whitaker – Played for 19 years, all with Detroit. Was the 1978 Rookie of the Year, a five-time All-Star, and a three-time Gold Glove winner at second base. In 1986, one of his All-Star seasons, he hit .269 with 20 home runs and 73 RBI.

Frank White – Played for 18 years, all with Kansas City. Played in five All-Star games, won eight Gold Gloves as a second baseman, and was the 1980 AL Championship Series MVP. In 1986, an All-Star season, he hit 22 home runs and 84 RBI, both career highs.

Mitch Williams – Pitched for six teams in 11 years. In his rookie year in 1986 with Texas, he was 8-6 with eight saves and a 3.58 ERA in 80 appearances, all in relief.

Ted Williams – Played his entire 19-year career with Boston as a left fielder and retired after the 1960 season. Finished with a .344 career batting average. Hit .406 in 1941 (he is still the last player to hit over .400) and hit under .300 just once in his career. Elected to the Hall of Fame in 1966.

Willie Wilson – An outfielder who played for 19 years, 15 of them with Kansas City. Had a .285 lifetime average. Stole 83 bases in 1979 and 668 for his career. Hit .269 and had 34 steals in 1986.

Dave Winfield – Played for 22 years with six teams, including with the New York Yankees in 1986 when he hit 24 home runs and had 104 RBI. Was a right fielder and 12-time All-Star who finished his career with 3,110 hits and 465 home runs. Elected to the Hall of Fame in 2001.

Steve Yeager – Played for 15 years with the Los Angeles Dodgers before spending his last season with Seattle in 1986 as a reserve catcher. Was the World Series MVP in 1981 and had the highest caught-stealing percentage among all catchers in the NL in 1978 and 1982.

Rich Yett – Pitched for Cleveland four of his six years in the league. In 1986, he made 39 appearances, all but three in relief. He went 5-3 with one save that season.

Robin Yount – The shortstop and center fielder played all 20 years with Milwaukee. Had 3,142 hits, won two league MVP awards, was the 1982 Major League Player of the Year, and was elected to the Hall of Fame in 1999. Hit .312 in 1986.

Statistics were gathered from www.baseball-reference.com.

www.ingramcontent.com/pod-product-compliance
Lightning Source LLC
LaVergne TN
LVHW051256080426
835509LV00020B/3009

हां, तुम
एक विजेता हो!

असीमित शक्ति का स्रोत-हमारा अवचेतन मन

आर. एस. चोयल

वी एण्ड एस पब्लिशर्स

प्रकाशक

वी एण्ड एस पब्लिशर्स

F-2/16, अंसारी रोड, दरियागंज, नई दिल्ली-110002
☎ 23240026, 23240027 • फ़ैक्स: 011-23240028
E-mail: info@vspublishers.com • *Website:* www.vspublishers.com

क्षेत्रीय कार्यालय : हैदराबाद

5-1-707/1, ब्रिज भवन (सेन्ट्रल बैंक ऑफ इण्डिया लेन के पास)
बैंक स्ट्रीट, कोटी, हैदराबाद-500 095
☎ 040-24737290
E-mail: vspublishershyd@gmail.com

शाखा : मुम्बई

जयवंत इंडस्ट्रिअल इस्टेट, 1st फ्लोर-108, तारदेव रोड
अपोजिट सोबो सेन्ट्रल, मुम्बई - 400 034
☎ 022-23510736
E-mail: vspublishersmum@gmail.com

फ़ॉलो करें:

ISBN 978-93-814487-5-5
संस्करण 2018

मुद्रक : रेप्रो नॉलेजकास्ट लिमीटेड, ठाणे